A Well-Watered Garden

A Gardener's Guide to Spirituality

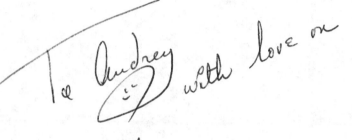

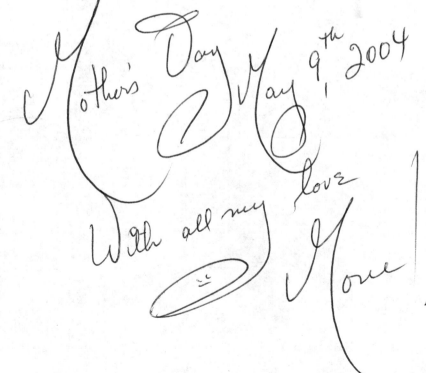

To Audrey, with love on Mother's Day May 9th, 2004

With all my love

Mom!

A Well-Watered Garden

A Gardener's Guide to Spirituality

HARRIET CROSBY

Thomas Nelson Publishers
NASHVILLE · ATLANTA · LONDON · VANCOUVER

Published in Nashville, Tennessee, by Thomas Nelson, Inc., Publishers, and distributed in Canada by Word Communications, Ltd., Richmond, British Columbia, and in the United Kingdom by Word (UK), Ltd., Milton Keynes, England.

Printed in the United States of America
1 2 3 4 5 6 7 — 01 00 99 98 97 96 95

For Smokey,
who showed me how.

Introduction

The Lord will guide you always;
he will satisfy your needs in a sun-scorched land
and will strengthen your frame.
You will be like a well-watered garden,
like a spring whose waters never fail.

ISAIAH 58:11 NIV

One October Sunday in 1991, I awoke to what promised to be an exceptionally hot day. I walked out on the deck of my home in the hills of Oakland, California, to view a cloudless sky and the sun dazzling the water of San Francisco Bay and the city beyond. With a spectacular view before me and a gorgeous day ahead, I thanked God that I lived in such a beautiful part of the country. I turned to look at the thermometer hanging on the wall. The temperature had already reached sixty-five degrees at seven o'clock in the morning. A warm breeze gently fanned my face. *Yes,* I thought to myself, *it's going to be a great day.*

By noon the temperature had soared into the upper nineties. The gentle breeze of the morning had turned into a blistering, fierce wind. I went out on my deck again. This time the view of San Francisco was blurred and hazy. I looked north over the hills and saw a dark cloud slowly moving toward my cottage. As I thought how odd it was to get rain in October, especially with such unusual heat, my landlord came out of his house and yelled up to me, "There's a six-alarm fire burning out of control in the hills. It's only a couple of miles away, and it's moving south. Turn on your radio."

I tuned in to a local station. What had begun the day before as a small brush fire in the hills near the Oakland/Berkeley border had turned into a fire that was blazing mightily, destroying homes and claiming lives. The fire had jumped the freeway and was heading south, toward my home.

During the next couple of hours, my landlord, neighbors, and I were glued to the radio while we watched the black cloud of smoke grow over us. Ash fell like rain. By three o'clock in the afternoon, the six-alarm fire became a "firestorm": a fire so fierce that it created its own weather. The temperature now registered well over one hundred degrees in the Oakland hills.

The radio announcer told us that the police had begun to evacuate our neighborhood, and my landlord suggested that we load up our cars with whatever we could carry and leave. We drove away expecting to lose our homes and everything we owned. But at least we left with our lives.

The next day my neighbors and I learned that we were lucky. Our homes had been spared—the fire had been contained a mile and a half to the north of us.

But three thousand people lost their homes and all of their possessions that night. Many of them were renters with no insurance. Twenty-six people also lost their lives.

Nine months later, some rebuilding had begun, but the fire area was still dominated by blackened, dead trees—most of the area remained scorched, with no vegetation at all. In the middle of the fire area, a community called the Hiller Highlands had been razed to the ground. Victims of the firestorm from there decided they wanted to create a monument to memorialize the loss of life and property, to be a symbol of hope and healing. They did not choose to build a monument of stone; instead they planted the Hiller Highlands Memorial Garden. Volunteers tend and water it on weekends. That garden has helped to heal an entire community. It is a well-watered garden, a living tribute to life and hope in the midst of a scorched land.

The Bible often uses gardens as symbols of healing and transformation. Isaiah 58 promises both to God's people when they behave justly toward their neighbors in need. In verse 11, the prophet wrote that out of the desolation and devastation of a sun-scorched land, the Lord will heal and strengthen the people, making them a well-watered garden, a source of life and nourishment to all who need them. This is one of the most beautiful promises in Scripture—out of all our pain and sorrow God will create a living garden of hope and healing. In the hands of the Lord, our pain will be transformed into a thing of beauty. And we will be renewed and strengthened, our souls nourished by springs of water that do not fail so that we can minister to our loved ones and our neighbors.

This theme runs throughout *A Well-Watered Garden*. You will plant, cultivate, and tend an actual garden as a way of seeing God at work transforming your life. This is *not* a gardening book, though it does offer tips on beginning a garden if you don't already have one. Through the coming year, you will explore your walk with the Lord using your garden as a place in which to think, reflect, pray, and experience the presence of God.

All too often we get so busy taking care of our families or ministering to friends and neighbors that our spiritual resources become drained and depleted. We need a regular time with God to nourish and strengthen our own souls. Your garden will provide a place to find refreshment, to seek nourishment from the Lord, and to walk with him in the cool of the day.

Your garden will also be a place of healing. You will discover that tending your garden is a way to seek healing from God, to transform pain into a thing of beauty and hope. Like the victims of the Oakland firestorm, you will find that caring for a living garden in the midst of pain and sorrow brings a slow, deep, and lasting healing.

My garden began with a package of catnip seeds a friend gave me to grow for my cat. I was unemployed at the time, and my life was undergirded by anxiety about the future; I found it difficult at that time to keep my spirits up.

I had never planted anything before because I had always lived in an apartment. But I planted the catnip in two little pots and put them in the sun on my deck. Every morning I watered the seeds and examined their progress. I began to realize that cultivating these seeds distracted me from my worries about the future. Caring for them each morning helped me to begin the day on a positive, hopeful note. Slowly, I began to see that by planting and tending my catnip seeds, I had trusted God with the future. I discovered that God, who brings life out of seeds, also brings joy out of despair.

Anyone who is unemployed will tell you that the pain of anxiety is often fed by feelings of failure. My little catnip seeds offered me the opportunity to combat those feelings. As the seeds slowly grew into full-sized plants, I realized I was a successful gardener. And, I said to myself, if I can see God at work in catnip plants, just think what I can learn from God with a whole garden!

Before long, I bought two different kinds of lavender, planted them in clay pots, and set them on my deck. They flourished! Heady with success, I decided to grow other fragrant herbs as well. Before long, I had an herb garden growing in a dozen different clay pots. I bought a book on growing and using herbs to help answer my beginner's questions. I now grow four different kinds of lavender, lemon verbena, scented geraniums, lemon balm, chamomile, and of course catnip. My garden continues to grow. And I have experienced transformation as God turned a painful time in my life into a time filled with promise and hope.

Getting Started

During biblical times, gardens were usually enclosed by stone or brick walls or by hedges with entrance gates that could be locked. Plants were grown as a source of food as well as for decoration. Gardens often became the sites of social gatherings. They were also used as places for meditation and prayer, and ancestral tombs were generally located in gardens.†

You will explore the connections between how you use your garden

---

†Paul J. Achtemeier, general editor, *Harper's Bible Dictionary* (San Francisco: Harper & Row, 1985), 332–33.

and how the gardens in Bible times were used. And you will explore the connections between your "outer" garden, the physical place, and your "inner" garden, that place in your heart where God heals and transforms you into the image of Christ. You will use your outer garden for social gatherings as well as a place for quiet reflection and prayer. And you will cultivate your inner garden, learning about death, resurrection, and life in Christ.

But first, you must begin. If you already have a garden growing at your home, you may want to skip to "A Prayer of Dedication." The remainder of this section is for first-time gardeners.

You do *not* need to live in a home with a big yard to grow a garden and explore your walk with God. Gardens can be as small as one potted plant or as large as a farm. You can become a successful gardener, even if you have never grown a plant in your life. Lots of wonderful plants are tough enough to survive a beginning gardener.

First, assess how much space you have for your garden. If you live in an apartment, your garden may be a couple of pots that occupy a windowsill. If you live in a house with a yard, choose a portion of the yard.

Once you have a general idea of where your garden will grow, observe the patterns of sun and shade for a couple of days. If your garden will live indoors, try to find space for your plants near a window. Does the window get direct or indirect sunlight? How much or how little sun your garden gets will determine the kinds of plants you can grow there.

For example, I rent a small cottage that has a shallow deck that stretches its length. Because my indoor space is limited, I decided my garden would live in clay pots on my deck. It faces due west, overlooking San Francisco Bay, and it gets full sun in the afternoon. But as I began to think about my garden and observe the light patterns on my deck, I noticed for the first time that a large oak tree growing by the side of the cottage partially shaded it each afternoon. I realized I could raise plants that need shade as well as those that prefer lots of sun.

Before you go trotting off to your local nursery or garden center, ask yourself, "What kind of garden do I want to grow?" This is where you can dream and let your imagination run wild. There are many different kinds of gardens you can grow: vegetable gardens, flower gardens, herb gardens. Some people grow theme gardens: Shakespeare gardens (plants found in Shakespeare's plays), Bible gardens (plants found in the Bible), night-blooming gardens, English gardens, French gardens, romantic gardens, Victorian gardens. If your garden will grow indoors, you have a wide variety of houseplants and herbs from which to choose.

I decided to plant an herb garden because many herbs are hardy and easy to grow. Several herbs also grow well as indoor plants, and I wanted to bring a few of my pots inside the cottage during the winter months. Many people grow culinary herbs to use in their cooking. I'm a terrible cook, so I avoided culinary herbs and instead chose herbs whose leaves and flowers make good potpourri indoors or perfume the air outside my door.

To help stir your imagination about these and many other possibilities, go to your local library and skim through several books about gardens and gardening. Most of these books are full of beautiful color photographs. But be careful—looking through these gorgeous books can whip you into a frenzy of horticultural excitement!

Now it's time to head to your local nursery or gardening center. You know about how much space you have. You've observed how much sunlight is available for your future garden. You're excited because you want your garden to look like all those gardens in the library books.

However, there are a couple of other factors that will determine what kind of garden you can successfully plant—the climate and soil conditions where you live. This is where talking to someone at your local nursery comes in. Seasons and general climate will ultimately determine the kind of garden you can grow. For example, at the time of this writing, California is in the midst of a six-year drought. Many people are choosing to plant gardens that have only drought-resistant plants. Local nursery workers know what plants thrive under drought conditions.

You may live in an area of the country that has four distinct seasons. Each season determines when you can plant or sow and what plants you can grow. Ask at your local nursery for help in selecting plants that will thrive and flourish during each season of the year.

I planted my herb garden in the summertime, and I came across a package of annual chamomile seeds that said the seeds must be sown only in the spring. Afraid I was too late, I asked at my nursery whether those directions applied to California. I learned that most seed packet directions are for parts of the country with four distinct seasons. The Bay Area only has two relatively mild seasons (winter and summer), and I could sow seed virtually any time of the year, especially in autumn just before the winter rains begin.

Choose plants suitable for the kind of soil in your area. Of course, if you choose to plant an indoor garden, simply purchase good-quality potting soil.

When you shop for your plants, find someone at the gardening center who is patient in answering the kinds of questions all beginning gardeners ask. Make friends with this person. The one who answered my question about chamomile seeds took the time to be helpful—even though my total purchase was only $1.76 for the seed! When I have questions about my herb garden, I can seek her out and she is happy to help me. Your local nursery workers will be invaluable resources in helping you purchase plants wisely and in helping you grow and tend a beautiful garden.

Don't feel you need to buy all of the plants at once for the garden of your dreams. I recommend you select only a few, plant them, see how they look, and determine how easy they are to cultivate. Let a few weeks go by before returning to your nursery to purchase a few more plants. Building your garden slowly offers you the opportunity to experiment with a variety of plants that complement or contrast with others in your garden. And building your garden a few plants at a time prolongs the pleasure of planning, dreaming, planting, and generally tinkering with your garden.

A few inexpensive tools will help you plant and tend your garden:

- A shovel to prepare the soil for planting
- A hand fork to help weed your garden
- A hoe for planting and weeding (especially useful with large vegetable gardens)
- Pruning shears for large shrubs and plants
- A hose long enough to bring water from the outdoor faucet to your garden
- An all-purpose fertilizer

If you have a smaller garden or, like me, a garden growing in pots, the following may be all you need:

- A hand trowel
- Pots and potting soil
- An all-purpose fertilizer
- A watering can

If you have any questions about which tools you need for your garden, don't be shy about asking for help.

Planting Your Garden

You've returned from the nursery triumphant with a few carefully chosen plants and tools. Now it's time to plant your garden. The size of your garden will, of course, determine how long it takes to plant it. But whether you're potting one plant or sowing a vegetable garden, take your time and enjoy the experience.

Most activities require that we finish tasks as quickly and efficiently as possible. Our families expect meals on time; projects often have tight deadlines; and church activities, other commitments, and play get squeezed into the remaining time.

Before you begin planting, clear some space on your calendar. Your garden is *not* another project to be finished on time. Your garden is a special place where you *slow down*, reflect on your life, and listen as God speaks to you. Plant your garden with reverence.

- Take time to feel the earth in your hands—it is the same earth out of which God created humankind.

- Look carefully at the plants you are putting into the dirt—allow yourself to experience the wonder of life you hold in your hands.

- Take time in between planting each plant and enjoy God's creation through all of your senses (if you are planting indoors, open a window): listen to the birds; smell the freshly dug earth; feel the sun warm your body; observe the colors of sky and earth.

- Notice any tender feelings you may have toward your garden as you carefully water each new plant—you are now God's steward of this plot.

Remember, you are creating a garden, a place to walk with God.

A Prayer of Dedication

Your garden is a sacred place. As you use this book throughout the coming weeks and months, you will meet God there. It is important, therefore, to offer your garden to God and ask that God's blessing rest upon it. Whether you have just finished planting your first pot or you already have acres growing, pray the following prayer of dedication.

Lord, into your hands I offer my garden and myself. Bless each plant; make my garden flourish and thrive. Bless me, O God. Strengthen me to be a faithful steward of this garden. Bless each person who visits this space, Lord. May each one find you here. And Lord, throughout the

coming weeks and months meet me here. Use my garden to speak to me,
nourish me, and heal me. For I pray in the name of Jesus Christ.
Amen. 🙠

Using This Book in Your Garden

The meditations on Scripture and exercises in this book are designed
to help you find nourishment, healing, and transformation from the
Lord as you tend your garden. By caring for your garden, you will
explore the many ways God is at work making your life and ministry a
well-watered garden.

This book is divided into the fifty-two weeks of the year. Each
week offers a Bible reading, a brief reflection on it, and a prayer. There
are also exercises based on the Scripture reading and reflection. Each
exercise will help you explore your walk with God in your actual outer
garden as well as in your spirit, your inner garden. As you tend your
outer garden with love and care, you learn to tend the inner garden of
your soul in response to God's love and grace. Each week you will find
two sections labeled Outer Garden and Inner Garden in which to write
your responses to the exercise. Occasionally an exercise may prompt
you to explore an aspect of your spiritual life in more detail. Should
you find you need more space in which to write your responses, continue writing in a journal or blank book and keep it handy as you work
your way through the year.

Suggestions for Enhancing Your Garden

Make the most of your garden—it is much, much more than a collec-
tion of growing things. It is a place where you will walk with God, a
special place that will refresh you, where God will bring healing and
transformation to your life and ministry. Decorate it, experiment with
it, lavish attention on it so that when you enter your garden you will
know you've entered holy ground.

Following are a few things I use to enhance my garden. These items won't make your plants and flowers grow better, but they may help make your garden more restful. Perhaps you can think of other ways to create a more beautiful, holy place. Only your imagination will limit what you can do to make your garden an enjoyable place in which to meet with God.

Wind chimes. Wind chimes come in a wide variety of sizes, shapes, and musical tones. I have a set in my herb garden. When the air stirs the chimes, I am reminded that the Holy Spirit continually moves over the face of the earth like the breeze. The gentle sound reminds me that God walks with me in my garden. Consider hanging a set of wind chimes from a tree in your garden. If you have an indoor garden, you can hang a set in front of an open window during the summer months.

A personal teapot and teacup. Set aside a teapot and teacup to use only in your garden. I have a single-serving teapot with a matching teacup that stores upside-down on top of it. As I brew my tea, the heat from the water in the pot warms the cup. I only use my special set when writing in my journal or sitting quietly in my herb garden. I find drinking a soothing cup of herb tea puts me in a reflective state of mind and quiets my soul for prayer. And seeing my teapot and teacup reminds me that I am entering my garden to spend time with God. Spending a quiet half-hour sipping a cup of tea, listening for the still, small voice of God in the breezes that blow over your garden is incredibly refreshing and comforting.

A chair and small table. I find a comfortable chair helps me to relax and admire my garden. I have placed a small, green, Parisian cafe table with two matching chairs on my deck next to my herb garden, where I can write in my journal comfortably. The table also easily holds my teapot and teacup. This setup affords enough room to share tea or dinner with a friend. In this way, I can occasionally share the beauty and fragrance of my herb garden.

Garden statuary or fountains. Many people find garden statuary or ornaments add to the restfulness of their gardens. Statues come in all sizes and shapes. And fountains add the soothing sound of gently splashing water. I would love to add a fountain to my herb garden, but most filled fountains are too heavy for my deck. Your local garden center will have a variety of garden statuary and fountains to choose from.

Bird feeders and baths. Consider adding a bird feeder and/or bath to your garden. Both come in a variety of sizes. I hang a plastic feeder for small birds right outside a window under the eaves of my cottage. It attracts finches and others to my herb garden and entertains my cat, who spends hours sitting in the window tantalized by all those busy birds.

If you have an indoor garden, feeders are available with suction cups that attach to the outside of your window. Small birds virtually perch on your window and bring the outdoors closer to your indoor garden.

A bird bath is a less expensive alternative to a fountain that both adds the restful presence of water to your garden and attracts birds.

Animals make any garden come alive. The presence of finches in my garden always reminds me of the kingdom of God in Jesus' parable of the mustard seed: the seed "grew and became a tree, and the birds of the air perched in its branches" (Luke 13:19 NIV).

Remember, these are only suggestions. Dream about your garden and find creative ways to make it feel beautiful and unique.

A Blessing

You have begun to create a holy place, a garden where you can walk with God in the cool of the day. After all, that is what God created us to do—to enjoy the presence of his company in a beautiful garden. May your walk with God in your special garden spot heal your spirit and soothe your soul.

A Well-Watered Garden

A Gardener's Guide to Spirituality

Spring

Spring

The kingdom of heaven is like treasure hidden in a field, which someone found and hid; then in his joy he goes and sells all that he has and buys that field.

MATTHEW 13:44 NRSV

Sometimes our gardens' hidden treasures make gardening a joy. Volunteer plants that pop up from nowhere one morning can add pleasure to our gardens. My landlord called me one spring morning to come see the volunteers in his garden—a sweeping carpet of sweet-smelling violets—that had bloomed the night before. He didn't plant them. A few had appeared a couple of years earlier and every year since more and more had returned. Their fragrance filled the air, and their deep purple color made a beautiful contrast to the other flowers growing near them.

The birth, death, and resurrection of Jesus Christ brought the kingdom of heaven to earth. Like my landlord's violets, the kingdom of heaven is hidden everywhere in everyday places—in a field or in the beauty of a garden. The kingdom of heaven is all around us; all we have to do is look for it. It awaits detection in our hearts, the eyes of someone we love, the work we do, the songs of praise we sing, the prayers we pray.

Week 1

Exercise:

Are there surprises in your garden this week? What blessings are there as a sign of the kingdom of heaven? Look for God's kingdom in your garden this week and record what you find in the Outer Garden column.

Seek the kingdom of heaven as you go about your routine this week. Look for surprises, especially hidden blessings. The kingdom of heaven is near. Record the signs of the kingdom of heaven in the Inner Garden section.

Lord, your kingdom surrounds me. Open to me the kingdom of heaven that I may live in peace. Open my eyes to recognize other inhabitants of your kingdom that I may know and love them. In Jesus' name. Amen.

Outer Garden

Inner Garden

Spring

Shepherd your people with
your staff,
the flock that belongs to
you,
which lives alone in a
forest
in the midst of a garden
land;
let them feed in Bashan
and Gilead
as in the days of old.

MICAH 7:14 NRSV

There is a tenderness to this verse that touches me deeply. A shepherd feeding his flock alone in a "garden land" is the very image of peace and quietness. There is a gentleness to Micah's scene that softens our hearts.

Galatians 5:23 records *gentleness* as one of the fruits of the Spirit. The world will recognize us as God's people by how gentle we are with ourselves, with Christians, and with those who don't know the Lord. Too often we look for evidence of the presence of God's Spirit in miracles, answers to prayer, good works, righteousness, and so forth. These things do point to the presence of the Holy Spirit, but all too often we overlook the experience of simple gentleness as a sign of the Spirit's presence.

Our gardens can teach us about the experience of gentleness. As a shepherd gently tends his flock, so we gardeners gently tend our gardens. With infinite patience we lavish care and precious time cultivating a beautiful place, pleasing to God and those we love. That same patience and care can be given to family and friends—and to ourselves as we seek to grow gently into the image of Christ.

Week 2

Exercise:

Spring planting can help us experience gentleness. Placing seedlings into the ground or sowing tiny seeds requires a gentle touch, as does the handling of all small, living things. Then comes the feeding and watering—*gently*, so as not to wash away the soil. As you plant your spring garden, let gentleness be in your mind and heart. Pay attention to your experience of this fruit of the Spirit and record your experience in the Outer Garden section.

Spend this week noticing moments of gentleness—that you show to yourself or to others. Also pay attention to how someone may be gentle with you. The Spirit is near. Record in the Inner Garden section these moments of gentleness and how you felt the presence of the Holy Spirit.

Gentle Jesus, too often I forget to look for you in gentleness and quiet. Help me to find you in a gentle touch, a look, a word. And help me find your Spirit in my garden that I may learn more of you. In Jesus' name. Amen.

Outer Garden

_____
_____
_____
_____
_____
_____
_____

Inner Garden

_____
_____
_____
_____
_____
_____
_____

Spring

So they took branches of palm trees and went out to meet him, shouting, "Hosanna! Blessed is the one who comes in the name of the Lord—the King of Israel!"

JOHN 12:13 NRSV

California is mostly desert, and the presence of its many palm trees reminds me that I live in a huge, human-made oasis. Palm trees have always symbolized the presence of water and life in the desert. They conjure up old movie images of a half-starved, thirst-driven man crawling across the hot dunes toward an oasis and the promise of life. Although palm trees grow year round in California, they are, like spring itself, a symbol of life.

In biblical times, the leaves of the palm were symbols of joy and celebration, in part because they indicated the presence of water in the desert and partially because of the dates they produced for food. To a people half-starved and thirst-driven for a Messiah, the presence of palm branches at Jesus' entry into Jerusalem was entirely appropriate. The palm branches pointed to Jesus, the One who would make Jerusalem an oasis in a brutal, pagan world.

Exercise:

We may not all have palm trees in our gardens, but chances are we do have trees growing there. If, like me, you have no backyard, you can certainly find trees in your neighborhood or a nearby park.

Week 3

If possible, do this exercise on Palm Sunday or sometime during Holy Week. Select a tree. Take a blanket and spread it under the tree close enough to the trunk so that you can lean your back on it. In the Outer Garden section describe the tree in detail; if possible, identify it by name.

As you lean against the tree, imagine its roots beneath you.

> ✢ How are you "rooted" in God? How does God feed and nourish your life?

Now feel the trunk you are leaning against. Imagine it as the center, the core of your life.

> ✢ What *is* the core of your life—spouse, children, church, close friends, work?

> ✢ How does God strengthen the core of your life with blessings?

Look up into the boughs and branches of the tree. See how they reach out or up to the sun.

> ✢ Spend some time in prayer. Let your prayers float up to nest in the branches of the tree and find rest before the King of Israel.

Later, record your experience under the tree in the Inner Garden section.

O King Eternal, you are my strength. You fill my life with so many blessings of family and friends and other good things. As the palm branches once celebrated your coming, let my prayers celebrate your presence. In your name, I pray. Amen. ✢

Outer Garden

_____

_____

_____

_____

_____

_____

_____

_____

_____

Inner Garden

_____

_____

_____

_____

_____

_____

_____

_____

Spring

For you shall go out in
joy,
and be led back in peace;
the mountains and the
hills before you
shall burst into song,
and all the trees of the
field shall clap their
hands.
Instead of the thorn shall
come up the cypress;
instead of the brier shall
come up the myrtle;
and it shall be to the
LORD for a memorial,
for an everlasting sign
that shall not be cut
off.

ISAIAH 55:12–13 NRSV

Isaiah recorded a beautiful promise from God to Israel in exile. Spring will finally come to a people who have endured a long, harsh winter of oppression and captivity. All of creation—mountains and hills, the trees in the fields—will rejoice when God's people are led back into their own land. Not only that, but the new growth of myrtle and cypress, where once grew only the thorns and brier of misery and pain, also stands as a memorial, a promise that the people of God will never be exiled again.

Spring is the season of promise, the season of Easter. I vividly remember the first day of spring last year. It was a beautiful, crystal-blue day in March. The breeze was cool, but the sun was finally warm again. I took my table and chairs out to my little garden on the deck. As I sat down, I felt a tremendous lift to my spirits, as though a long-closed door had opened in my heart. I looked out over the San Francisco Bay and could imagine the Spirit of God moving over the face of the water. I thought to myself, *Soon the skyscrapers in the city will clap their hands!* The long, rainy winter was over. Spring had come, and Easter would soon arrive with its promise of resurrection and the reign of the kingdom of God.

Week 4

Exercise:

Like the trees Isaiah wrote about, our gardens are signs of promise. As you work in your garden this week, identify those plants and flowers that hold the most promise for summer and harvest. Record these plants and flowers in the Outer Garden section.

The Easter season promises that God's people will be led out of the captivity of sin and death's exile. Let your garden be a memorial to you that the time of captivity and exile are over in the death and resurrection of Jesus Christ. This week, as you work in your garden, keep this book and a pen or pencil nearby. Meditate on the promise of Easter as you work away; reflect on how God is leading you out of captivity this Easter. In the Inner Garden section:

- ❧ Jot down any feelings you have.

- ❧ Write any verses that come to mind.

- ❧ Record your thoughts and reflections about this Easter.

All praise and thanks to you, O Christ, who has led me out of sin's captivity and death's dark exile. Your word is like a life-giving stream that never fails. Guide me as I meditate on your Scriptures this week. Your law, O Lord, I love. In Jesus' name. Amen. ❧

Outer Garden

_____

_____

_____

_____

_____

_____

_____

_____

Inner Garden

_____

_____

_____

_____

_____

_____

_____

_____

$Spring$

. . . What you sow does not come to life unless it dies. And as for what you sow, you do not sow the body that is to be, but a bare seed, perhaps of wheat or of some other grain.

1 CORINTHIANS
15:36–37 NRSV

We all know that the seeds we sow in our gardens are dead until we water them and ensure they have the right amount of sunlight. I remember the first nasturtium I planted in a pot. It thrived all summer then began to die back in the late fall. But it left behind many large seeds, which I eventually planted in a small patch of ground behind my cottage. Out of those dead, dry seeds, several huge nasturtium plants grew and bloomed.

Paul tried to communicate the mystery of death and resurrection using an image from the garden. We know what kind of plants the seeds we sow in our garden will produce, but our physical, earthly bodies sown in death will become resurrected bodies raised in glory that we can't know about ahead of time. Paul goes on in verse 42 to write, "What is sown is perishable, what is raised is imperishable" to give the Corinthians some idea of how surprisingly different resurrection will be.

This spring, as we sow seeds in our gardens, we can meditate on Christ's death and resurrection—and our own.

Week 5

Exercise:

This week, read 1 Corinthians 15. Take the time to absorb its message. It is one of the great chapters in the Bible. Select two or three verses and memorize them. Write the verses you will memorize in the Inner Garden section.

Find a place in your garden where you can plant a few seeds. When weather and ground conditions permit, sow the seeds and meditate on the verses you are memorizing from 1 Corinthians 15. Reflect especially on how those verses shape your understanding of your own death and resurrection. Record what kind of seeds you planted and the day you did so in the Outer Garden section.

Lord, you are God of the resurrection. Help me to enjoy the mystery of death and resurrection. Let me ever trust that one day I will awaken to behold your glory in your kingdom. In your name, I pray. Amen.

Outer Garden

_____

_____

_____

_____

_____

_____

_____

_____

_____

Inner Garden

_____

_____

_____

_____

_____

_____

_____

_____

Spring

And I will appoint a place for my people Israel and will plant them, so that they may live in their own place, and be disturbed no more; and evildoers shall afflict them no more.

2 SAMUEL 7:10 NRSV

Many of us regard our gardens as a sanctuary. We can go there to get away from the disturbance of the telephone or family demands for a little while and lose ourselves in tending our gardens.

When I'm potting new plants on a fine spring day, my deck is transformed. I hear the birds' songs and the sound of my wind chimes as they stir gently in a spring breeze. I know that God has appointed this place for me. As soon as I saw it in my search for a home, I knew beyond a doubt that this was the place God intended me to live. Not long after I moved in, I experienced dark, troubled times. God knew that I would need a sanctuary during this storminess. And my home, especially my herb garden on the deck, has been a sanctuary every day.

Israel, too, longed for a sanctuary in which to live, a place where they could enjoy the mercy of God. As God's people, we seek sanctuary in our gardens, homes, families, and other relationships.

Week 6

Exercise:

As you work in your garden this spring, meditate on 2 Samuel 7:10. How has God planted you in your own place? How is it a sanctuary for you? How has God protected you with his mercy from evildoers? Record the fruit of your meditation in the Inner Garden section. In the Outer Garden section, record what you have planted this year.

Lord, you have given me sanctuary in my own place. You have covered me with your mercy as the shade of a tree covers the ground underneath. I do not take my garden, my sanctuary, or your mercy for granted. They are signs of your grace and love. Accept my thanks and praise, O Lord. In Jesus' name. Amen.

Outer Garden

Inner Garden

Spring

Bear fruit worthy of repentance.

MATTHEW 3:8 NRSV

I have a T-shirt that reads, "Every garden counts." No garden is too small or insignificant, because any garden is a place where growth and beauty happen. The same is true of repentance. All too often we think of repentance as a painful experience. In fact, repentance is an invitation to new spiritual growth. Just as we cultivate our gardens, we are called by the Lord to cultivate repentance in our lives, to "bear fruit worthy of repentance." The fruit of repentance is freedom and joy. Repenting of sin or anything that keeps us from the Lord is liberating and a cause for rejoicing. Repentance prepares the ground of our souls for growth and beauty in the Spirit.

Week 7

Exercise:

Weeding is an excellent activity for reflecting on where in our lives God calls us to repentance. Just as weeding makes our gardens beautiful and gives our plants' and flowers' roots more space to grow, identifying areas where we need to make room in our hearts helps us begin the process of growth as Christians.

Set aside an hour this week for weeding in your garden. As you do so, ask God where you need to repent and grow. Also pray for God's strength and grace to bear fruit worthy of your repentance. Write in the Inner Garden section about where you feel called to repent in your life. In the Outer Garden section, record that you weeded and write your observations regarding your garden's beauty.

Lord, I thank you for showing me where I need to repent and turn again to your love and grace. I cannot bring about repentance on my own by strength of will; I need to experience the power of your love to return me again to you. Give me the grace, O Christ, to bear the fruit of freedom and rejoicing, fruit worthy of repentance. Amen.

Outer Garden

_____

_____

_____

_____

_____

_____

_____

_____

Inner Garden

_____

_____

_____

_____

_____

_____

_____

_____

Spring

The flowers appear on the earth;

the time of singing has come,

and the voice of the turtledove

is heard in our land.

SONG OF SOLOMON
2:12 NRSV

Spring lifts my heart. Suddenly everything is in bloom. I thrill at birds' songs I missed all winter. As I sit on my deck, my own small Eden, and smell the fragrance of my herb garden warmed by the sun and listen to the birds sing, everything feels new and clean. The days grow longer and warmer, and the last place I want to be is indoors.

Spring is God's way of celebrating, of telling the world how much he loves all of creation. Gardeners know this great spiritual truth. As our gardens become increasingly lush, we can't help but praise the beauty of God's creation. With spring, "the time of singing has come."

Week 8

Exercise:

Invite a few friends to your garden, and ask them to bring their Bibles. You may want to offer refreshments to make the occasion a celebration of spring. When everyone has gathered, sit in the garden and begin your time together by explaining that the psalms in the Bible are songs of praise and prayer. Ask your guests to choose a favorite psalm and to share with the group what makes their psalm special to them. You may want to close your time together by singing a couple of favorite hymns, which are contemporary psalms.

Record the highlights of your celebration in the Outer Garden section. Write about how the afternoon touched your soul in the Inner Garden section.

Our God, you are the Lord of all life. I give you thanks for your bountiful grace, which sustains and nourishes all of creation. The beauty of my garden in springtime lifts my soul in praise to you, O Lord! All praise, honor, and glory be unto you Father, Son, and Holy Spirit! Amen.

Outer Garden

_____

_____

_____

_____

_____

_____

_____

_____

_____

_____

Inner Garden

_____

_____

_____

_____

_____

_____

_____

_____

_____

_____

Spring

I will rejoice in doing good to them, and I will plant them in this land in faithfulness, with all my heart and all my soul.

JEREMIAH 32:41 NRSV

Just as we rejoice over the plants and flowers in our gardens, God rejoices over us. As gardeners, we lavish tender care on our gardens—planting, weeding, pruning, fertilizing. Using the image of God as the Great Gardener, Jeremiah told of the tenderness God has toward his people: "I will plant them in this land in faithfulness, with all my heart and all my soul." God rejoices in doing good to us, the descendants of God's covenant people.

Jeremiah wrote this verse to a people in trouble. When we walk through difficult times in our lives or walk with another in trouble, it's easy to forget that God rejoices in doing good in our lives and in those of the people we love. We can cling to this image of God the Great Gardener, who lavishes tender love and faithfulness on us with his heart and soul. When we experience a spiritual winter in the midst of spring, God is faithful, tenderly cultivating our souls that we may know the beauty of springtime in our hearts once again.

Week 9

Exercise:

If you or someone you love is experiencing a spiritual winter in the middle of springtime, find creative ways to bind this verse to your heart. Here are a few suggestions:

- Memorize Jeremiah 32:41.

- Write Jeremiah 32:41 on several strips of paper, and tie them with ribbon to trees or other plants in your garden. Offer them as praise and thanks to God for his goodness and faithfulness during this difficult time.

- Purchase an attractive blank card for a loved one going through a tough time. Write Jeremiah 32:41 and a prayer in the card. You may wish to pick a flower from your garden, press it, and include it in your card.

- Make a bookmark and write Jeremiah 32:41 on it. Place it in your Bible so you will be reminded of it during quiet times.

In the Inner Garden section, record how Jeremiah 32:41 has ministered to your wintry spirit this week. In the Outer Garden section, record how you used this verse.

Lord, though winter is in my heart, I open myself to the warmth of your faithfulness and tender care. Holy Spirit, blow warm spring winds through my soul. Let me rejoice with you once again. I believe that I will experience your love and goodness again soon. In Jesus' name. Amen.

Outer Garden

_____

_____

_____

_____

_____

_____

_____

_____

Inner Garden

_____

_____

_____

_____

_____

_____

_____

_____

Spring

[Jesus] said therefore, "What is the kingdom of God like? And to what should I compare it? It is like a mustard seed that someone took and sowed in the garden; it grew and became a tree, and the birds of the air made nests in its branches."

LUKE 13:18–19 NRSV

Jesus placed his parable of the mustard seed in the hands of a gardener. The gardener plants the seed, and the growth of the mustard tree is like the kingdom of God. God's reign on earth begins and continues in a garden.

My deck is built about ten feet off the ground, and it symbolizes the kingdom of God for me. When I'm in my deck garden, I feel like one of "the birds of the air" who has made her nest in a branch of God's kingdom. I've added a couple of special touches to remind me of the holiness of this sacred place. At one end of my deck I have a little terra-cotta Celtic symbol of the Trinity—three fish joined in a circle. At the other end, I put up a small ceramic figure of the risen Christ. I enjoy God's kingdom there—praying, reading, watching the sun set, entertaining friends, writing in my journal, or simply sitting quietly.

This spring, make your garden a holy place that reflects the presence of the kingdom of God.

Week 10

Exercise:

Make a list in the Outer Garden section of all the things you could do in your garden to make it a sacred place. Brainstorm and list as many things as you can. Then go back over your list and select three things and do them. When you have finished doing those three things, pray a prayer of rededication, asking God to help you remember that your garden is a holy place.

Jesus' parable of the mustard seed is really about how the kingdom of God takes root in God's people. This week, sit quietly in your garden and reflect on how the kingdom of God has been sown in your life. Record your reflections in the Inner Garden section.

Lord Jesus, make your kingdom grow in my garden and in my life. May all I do and all I am show the world that your kingdom lives in me to the glory of your name. Amen.

Outer Garden

_____

_____

_____

_____

_____

_____

_____

Inner Garden

_____

_____

_____

_____

_____

_____

_____

Spring

After Jesus had spoken these words, he went out with his disciples across the Kidron valley to a place where there was a garden, which he and his disciples entered. . . . Jesus often met there with his disciples.

JOHN 18:1–2 NRSV

Gardens in the Bible remind God's people of the original garden, Eden. They are oases in a desert wilderness, signs of God's love and mercy for his people in the midst of trial and difficulty in a fallen world. No wonder Jesus led his disciples just east of Jerusalem, across the Kidron valley to a favorite garden to pray during his greatest trial. For this is no ordinary gathering for prayer. Jesus knew that he would offer up his life in a matter of hours.

Our gardens, too, are oases of prayer. Just as Jesus did, we can offer up all of our troubles to our merciful and loving Lord in our gardens. I like to pray surrounded by the sight and smell of the thriving herbs and flowers that assure me of God's faithfulness. It's almost as though my garden releases prayer within me, and I pour out to the Lord all that is on my heart. In my own oasis of prayer, God reminds me that he is ever present, ever at work to redeem my life and this fallen world.

Week 11

Exercise:

This week, find or create a comfortable spot in your garden in which to pray. You may wish to take a heavy, old blanket outside to sit or kneel on—there is something special about praying while sitting or kneeling on God's own earth. In the Old Testament, God's people frequently marked a special encounter with him using rocks. Try arranging a few rocks in your garden to mark a particular meeting place with God. Experiment a bit to find the best spot in your garden for prayer.

Once you've identified the place that feels right, simply pray. Consider bringing along your Bible or this book or a prayer journal. Or you may want to simply bring yourself to meet God in your garden.

Later, record your experience of praying in your garden.

Lord, for this oasis of prayer, I give you thanks. For my garden shows me you are a merciful and loving God who is eager to meet me in prayer. Amen.

Outer Garden

Inner Garden

Spring

For as the earth brings
forth its shoots,
and as a garden causes
what is sown in it to
spring up,
so the Lord GOD will
cause righteousness and
praise
to spring up before all the
nations.

ISAIAH 61:11 NRSV

Isaiah used the image of a garden in springtime to give us an idea of the richness of God's righteousness and praise. After a long, dark winter, God's kingdom will burst forth like the new shoots and buds in a beautiful garden, bringing the feeling of freshness only springtime causes. It is a time of celebration in praise.

Again and again, biblical writers used the garden to tell us about God doing something brand new, just as he did in the original garden of Eden. ". . . Righteousness and praise [will] spring up before all the nations" and there will be a new creation.

The promise of that new creation, of Eden come once again to earth, thrills me every spring when the star jasmine buds begin to unfold. As they release their scent on the warm evening air, my heart sings with the knowledge that God is very, very good. At such a time, I find it impossible not to praise the goodness and wonder of God and his creation.

Week 12

Exercise:

This spring, as we watch our own gardens unfold into beautiful, rich places, God is calling us to celebrate the promise of his righteousness and praise. Take a daily walk through your garden during the week and keep a record in the Outer Garden section of the new flowers and plants you notice.

If you belong to a Bible study or a group at your church, invite the members to a spring garden party. Make the party as elaborate or as simple as you want. Ask your guests to come prepared with a story about their lives, families, church, or work that is cause to praise God. After each guest has shared a story, spend time praising and thanking God. Write your own story for the party in the Inner Garden section.

O Lord, I give you thanks for spring and all its promise of goodness from your hand. Give me eyes to see your kingdom in my garden, my life, my family, and our world. Give me the joy that comes of praising and thanking you. Amen. ❧

Outer Garden

_____

_____

_____

_____

_____

_____

_____

_____

Inner Garden

_____

_____

_____

_____

_____

_____

_____

Spring

For he has actually sent to us in Babylon, saying, "It will be a long time; build houses and live in them, and plant gardens and eat what they produce."

JEREMIAH 29:28 NRSV

It was the time of the long captivity. Israel was conquered and the most wise and talented of the people were sent by God to Babylon. In addition to building homes, God also told them to plant gardens that would help them to survive captivity.

The same God who led Israel into captivity blessed them with gardens to grow and food to eat.

Many of us have experienced being sent by God to a place we did not want to go. A few years ago, God led me out of a relationship with a man whom I loved. For a long time I was held captive by my feelings of loss and loneliness. But my personal captivity was lightened by my garden. Just as Israel planted gardens to survive in Babylon, I found gardening helped me to survive the loss of a love. Now I can see that God, who led me into a place I did not want to go, is the One who helped me to survive and heal in my garden.

Week 13

Exercise:

In the Inner Garden section, describe a time in your life when you were faced with surviving an illness or a loss of some kind.

Then enter your garden and record in the Outer Garden section the role, if any, that your garden played in your survival.

Describe your memorial plant in the Outer Garden section. Also write about your reasons for choosing this particular plant: does this kind of plant hold any special meaning for you? In the Inner Garden section write about what, or who, your plant memorializes in your life.

Lord, there have been times you have led me where I did not want to go. Sometimes you led me into a better place. Sometimes you led me into a place of captivity. But you are my Savior and will lead me, in the end, to live and love with you. In Jesus' name. Amen.

Outer Garden

_____

_____

_____

_____

_____

_____

_____

_____

_____

Inner Garden

_____

_____

_____

_____

_____

_____

_____

Spring

Like Adam, our first father, we are made to be gardeners. We may have friends and family who don't enjoy gardening; the primal urge to till and keep a garden has grown faint for many. But for us that urge remains—we just can't wait to grow things!

Throughout the many months I've tended my garden, I have looked for a home to buy. I want to transplant my container garden into the ground and begin to create an English garden. Recently, I toured a small house with a small backyard—which is completely covered with flagstone and concrete! I would love to get a jackhammer and break up all that concrete, remove it, and get down to the serious joy of creating a garden. My urge to garden is very strong. I want to tear up that urban patio and return to Eden.

And maybe that's what the primal urge is really all about. Each of us, in our own way, is trying to get back to our original home—Eden, the home God intended for us.

Week 14

Exercise:

While working in your garden this week, reflect on how your garden is your home. We often think of our houses as our homes. But in what ways is your garden an extension of that feeling of "home"? Record your answers in your Inner Garden section.

In the Outer Garden section, record the work you did in your garden this week.

Lord, I give you thanks for making me at home in my garden. I eagerly look forward to the day when all of your saints can join you in that heavenly Eden, our one true home. Until then, O Lord, I offer my life, my loves, my home into your loving care. Amen.

Outer Garden

_____

_____

_____

_____

_____

_____

_____

_____

Inner Garden

_____

_____

_____

_____

_____

_____

_____

Spring

*They shall again live
beneath my shadow,
they shall flourish as a
garden;
they shall blossom like the
vine,
their fragrance shall be
like the wine of
Lebanon.*

HOSEA 14:7 NRSV

God's promises are sometimes *lush*. Under the shade of God's shadow, God's people will once again "*flourish* as a garden" and "*blossom* like the vine"; "their *fragrance* shall be like the wine of Lebanon" (my italics). This verse elicits an image of an incredibly fragrant garden thriving, growing, every plant blooming. It is a cool and pleasant place. After a long time of deprivation and captivity, God's people will become beautiful once again.

Beauty is important to God, who cares deeply about the inner beauty of his people. As the people of God, we are to be like that lush and fragrant garden. But our beauty is more than skin deep; God cares about the beauty of our community life and the beauty of our souls. The life of discipleship under the shadow of Jesus Christ is like the garden Hosea described. It has its own kind of lushness that pleases the eye of God; it is a fragrant offering to God of our spirits and life together.

Week 15

Exercise:

Go into your garden and find a comfortable place to sit. Spend ten minutes absorbing the beauty of your garden. Then get up and walk slowly around your garden for at least ten minutes. Let every detail in your garden enter each of your five senses. Pay attention to *how* your garden is beautiful to the eye, to the touch, to the ear, to the nose, even, if applicable, to the tongue. Describe the beauty of your garden in the Outer Garden section.

Reflect on your life of discipleship following Jesus. Think about your interior, spiritual life, the inner garden you cultivate under the shadow of Christ. How is it beautiful to God? Then think about your life among the community of believers. How is your community life beautiful to God? Record your reflections as specifically as possible in the Inner Garden section.

Lord God, under the shadow of your wings I take refuge. It is there, Lord, that I grow in discipleship by the grace of your Holy Spirit. I know I'm not perfect. But when I seek to follow you, my life becomes like a garden that pleases you with its beauty. Continue, O God, to help me to follow, love, and serve you. In Jesus' name. Amen.

Outer Garden

_____
_____
_____
_____
_____
_____
_____

Inner Garden

_____
_____
_____
_____
_____
_____
_____

Spring

I am a very results-oriented person. I like to be in control and make things happen—quickly! When I first planted my herb garden, I checked on its progress every day. I wanted immediate growth, immediate gratification. Of course, the more I demanded quick results from my garden, the less growth I saw. I could not see real growth when I obsessively measured each plant twice a day!

My herb garden taught me to take the long view of growth. It showed me that deep, lasting growth occurs slowly, over a long period of time. There is a difference between being obsessive and being faithful. Being faithful to my garden means tending and caring for it, providing the *conditions* for growth. I have no control over the results, the actual growth of my herbs. Like Paul, I plant. I water. But only God gives growth.

I learned the same lesson regarding my inner garden. I must be faithful—providing the *conditions* for spiritual growth by practicing the disciplines of prayer, Bible study, and worship. But it is God who brings about deep, lasting spiritual growth. And that takes a long time, often a lifetime. To subject my spirit to obsessive, constant measurement robs me of the joy of God's grace. God grows my spirit in his own time. And God has plenty of time. Because he takes the long view about my spiritual growth, so can I. This frees me from worry and placing obsessive demands on myself. That is the joy of grace.

Week 16

Exercise:

This week explore the experience of God's grace in your garden.

Set aside twenty minutes to sit quietly in your garden with this book open in your lap. Also bring a pen or pencil.

Take several long, deep breaths. Relax. Let go of thinking about what you have to do later. Be present to the presence of God in your garden.

For the next ten minutes, let your eyes wander over the various plants in your garden. As your eyes roam, ask yourself, "Where do I see God's grace at work in my garden?" Jot any answers that come to mind in the Outer Garden section.

Take five minutes to look over your garden and select one plant on which to let your eyes rest. Imagine that plant represents your Inner Garden. Ask yourself, "Where do I see God's grace at work in my spiritual life, my inner garden?" Write any answers that come to mind in the Inner Garden section of this book.

Spend the last five minutes in prayer, thanking God for the grace that is yours in Christ. Offer up any "results" or "measurements" you've been demanding of yourself lately. Ask God for the grace to let Christ grow your spirit. If you like, you may pray the following prayer.

Lord, for the ways in which you've graced my life this week, I give you thanks and praise. I especially thank you for growing my garden and my life. Give me the strength and wisdom to be faithful in tending both my outer and inner gardens. Keep me from doing your job, from trying to force growth to meet my private timetable. I offer up to you my need for quick results and my obsession with self-measurement. Help me to be gentle and patient with myself and my garden. For I pray in Jesus' name. Amen. ❧

Outer Garden

_____

_____

_____

_____

_____

_____

_____

_____

_____

_____

Inner Garden

_____

_____

_____

_____

_____

_____

_____

_____

_____

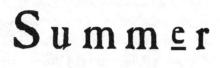

Summer

Summer

A garden locked is my
sister, my bride,
a garden locked, a
fountain sealed.
Your channel is an
orchard of
pomegranates
with all choicest fruits,
henna with nard,
nard and saffron,
calamus and
cinnamon,
with all trees of
frankincense,
myrrh and aloes,
with all chief spices—
a garden fountain, a well
of living water.

SONG OF SOLOMON
4:12–15 NRSV

God made gardens to delight our human senses. Here Solomon compared his bride to a garden rich in beauty, scent, taste, and even sound. Solomon sang about such a garden because it expressed the sensual delight he found in his bride. He particularly sang of the garden fountain. Its water is a symbol of life—the fountain is a "well of living water" that makes all growing things thrive. Garden fountains can please the eyes and especially the ears. We can almost hear the water in Solomon's song gurgling and bubbling, bringing life to a rich, exotic garden.

I love a garden with a pond or running water in it. Somehow its presence makes the beauty and even the scent of the flowers more intense. If there is a place to sit near water in a public garden or a friend's backyard, that is the spot where I choose to sit and let all of my God-given senses absorb the beauty of the place. And water in the garden reminds me of the "living water," the grace and mercy of God that flows without end, giving abundant life.

Exercise:

Not all of us can have a fountain or pond in our gardens. But we can enjoy the presence of water in our gardens anyway.

If you have an outdoor garden, find or buy a large container to hold water. It may be a shallow, broad terra-cotta pot, a lightweight wooden tub, or a large inverted lid from a garbage can—use anything that will hold enough water to resemble a small pond.

Week 17

Next, place the container in your garden where water will enhance its beauty. If the container itself is not very attractive, try to put it where plants partially hide it or partially bury it. You may want to put some large rocks in the bottom to give it a more natural, pond-like look. Then fill the container with water. You may wish to float flowers or candles on top of the water. [*Note:* For the purpose of this exercise, this outdoor pond is temporary. Standing water eventually attracts mosquitoes.]

If you have an indoor garden or a container garden on a deck or porch, use a large, shallow bowl or deep dish. Place it in the midst of your pots on a small stand or on a small table surrounded by some of your plants. You may wish to put small, ornamental rocks (available at most garden supply centers) on the bottom before filling it with water and floating small flowers or candles.

Spend time in your garden sitting near the water this week. Leave all the hustle and bustle of your life behind. Relax. Take deep breaths. Let all of your senses take in the beauty of your garden and little pond. As you do so, reflect on the following questions and record your thoughts here:

- Was this week's exercise a successful experience?

- How did the presence of water enhance the beauty of my garden?

- How did I experience the presence of Christ as "living water" this week?

Lord, your living water nourishes my soul, heals my heart during hard times, and strengthens me for ministry. I thank and praise you for the abundant life you pour out in me. Amen.

Outer Garden

Inner Garden

Summer

The Lord will guide you
always;
he will satisfy your needs
in a sun-scorched land
and will strengthen your
frame.
You will be like a
well-watered garden,
like a spring whose waters
never fail.

ISAIAH 58:11 NIV

In the Introduction I wrote about the 1991 firestorm in the Oakland/Berkeley hills. The Hiller Highlands Memorial Garden the survivors of the fire planted became a symbol of healing, hope, and promise in a "sun-scorched land."

God has blessed us with gardens for healing. When our lives become scorched by pain or adversity, our gardens remain living reminders of hope. Caring for our gardens is a concrete expression of our trust in the Lord of Life, who brings healing and growth. Our gardens teach us that our hope is in the Lord who satisfies all our needs. As we tend our gardens, we are assured that God is working in us, strengthening our frame, bringing healing out of pain, making us a well-watered garden in a sun-scorched land.

Exercise:

If your life has been scorched recently by trouble or pain, go to the nursery this week and purchase a special plant for your garden. Choose this new plant carefully—it will be your "memorial" plant. This plant will be a concrete expression of your hope in God. Whenever you tend this plant in your garden, you will remember to hope and pray for healing. When you bring your plant home, plant it in a special place in your garden. As you do so, pray the following prayer.

Week 18

Lord, I offer you this plant as a memorial to hope. Every time I care for this plant, help me to remember that you are the God of healing; help me to remember that my hope is in you. Lord, make this memorial plant flourish in my garden; make hope flourish in my heart. Strengthen me, O Lord, and make me a well-watered garden in a sun-scorched land. In Jesus' name I pray. Amen. ❧

If your life is relatively free of trouble or pain, you may still choose a "memorial" plant for your garden. Whenever you tend this plant, remember to give thanks to the God who makes you strong and gives you joy. As you put your plant in the soil, say the following prayer.

Lord, I offer you this plant as a memorial to strength and joy. When I tend this plant, help me to remember to give you thanks for strength and for those people who bring joy to my life; help me to remember that my hope is in you. Lord, make this plant flourish in my garden; make strength flourish in me; let it flow like a stream whose waters never fail. In Jesus' name I pray. Amen. ❧

Outer Garden

_____

_____

_____

_____

_____

_____

_____

_____

Inner Garden

_____

_____

_____

_____

_____

_____

_____

Summer

*He said to them, ". . .
For truly I tell you, if you
have faith the size of a
mustard seed, you will
say to this mountain,
'Move from here to there,'
and it will move; and
nothing will be impossible
for you."*

MATTHEW 17:20 NRSV

My whole garden started with my planting tiny catnip seeds. Eventually, one small seed grew into a bush three-and-a-half feet high and about three feet in diameter. And all the cats in the neighborhood now come to nest in its branches.

The mustard seed is one of the smallest seeds in the world. It takes very little faith to grow big miracles. But sometimes I find having even the smallest amount of faith the most difficult thing in the world—especially when times are hard. I recently experienced a series of painful losses. I found that simply having faith the size of a mustard seed became miracle enough, never mind moving mountains.

Jesus gave this teaching to a church experiencing severe trials and persecution. It is a teaching for the painful times in our lives, one that tells us to cultivate faith the size of a very tiny seed and let it grow in the ground of our own pain. Such faith sown in pain is a miracle great enough to move mountains.

Week 19

Exercise:

Go to your local nursery or garden supply store and browse the seed section. Purchase a packet of the smallest seeds you can find, and cultivate them in your garden. In your Outer Garden section, record the kind of seeds you planted, and make notes on their progress.

As you tend to your seeds, reflect on Jesus' teaching. Let the seeds symbolize your faith. Pay attention to what it takes for them to grow into healthy plants: good soil, careful watering, enough sunlight, and so on. Reflect as well on what it takes to cultivate/nurture your faith: Bible study, ministry, fellowship, and so forth. If you have been in any kind of emotional or physical pain, how can you grow your faith to the size of a mustard seed? How do you see your faith as a miracle? Quietly reflect on Jesus' teaching as it applies to your life and record your reflections in the Inner Garden section.

Lord Jesus, faith is a miracle you work in me. Let the gift of your faith sustain me through good times and bad times. May the faith I have, whether small or large, work miracles in me, in those I love, and in those you love. Whatever faith I have, I offer to the glory of your name. Amen.

Outer Garden

_____

_____

_____

_____

_____

_____

_____

_____

Inner Garden

_____

_____

_____

_____

_____

_____

_____

Summer

And the slaves of the householder came and said to him, "Master, did you not sow good seed in your field? Where, then, did these weeds come from?"

MATTHEW 13:27 NRSV

How many times have we stood in the middle of our gardens with hands on our hips exclaiming, "Where did these weeds come from?" After all, we're good gardeners; we don't deserve these weeds. Then we shake our heads and get down to the business of pulling them.

In Matthew 13:29–30 Jesus told his disciples that sometimes for good plants to flourish some weeds must be left alone lest the good plants get torn out with the weeds.

Occasionally, I weed the plot of land behind my cottage. I have to decide in certain cases when it's best to leave a weed so as not to accidentally pull up a plant or flower. I find I must be particularly discriminating when weeding around California poppies—it's often easy for me to confuse the weeds with young plants, so I let the weeds remain a while.

God is also discerning about letting some "weeds" stay in our selves, churches, and communities. We may be frustrated by the presence of sin in our lives. When we see people doing bad things to good people, it seems there is no justice. Yet we also know that in our lives (and the lives of others) our greatest weaknesses may also be the flip side of our greatest strengths. God the wise gardener knows when it's time to pull the weeds and when it's best to leave them growing among the good seed.

Week 20

Exercise:

The next time you weed your garden, think about how you make the decision to let some weeds live while you pull others. Record your thoughts in the Outer Garden section.

After you have finished weeding your garden, reflect on how your weaknesses (your personal weeds) support your strengths. Also examine your church and your community—what are their weaknesses, and how do those weaknesses lend strength or character to your church/community? Reflect, too, on why God might be leaving these tensions to grow. For example, I live in a city with a fairly high crime rate. But I also live in a city with great cultural and ethnic diversity. Many different kinds of people and cultures living together can create the tensions that cause crime. Record your thoughts in the Inner Garden section.

Lord, sometimes I feel choked by the weeds of my own sin and weakness. Sometimes I see weeds threatening to choke my church and community. Help me to trust you with the weeds. And protect, O Lord, the goodness that also abounds. In Jesus' name. Amen.

Outer Garden

_____

_____

_____

_____

_____

_____

_____

_____

_____

Inner Garden

_____

_____

_____

_____

_____

_____

_____

_____

Summer

. . . We have not ceased praying for you and asking that you may be filled with the knowledge of God's will in all spiritual wisdom and understanding, so that you may lead lives worthy of the Lord, fully pleasing to him, as you bear fruit in every good work and as you grow in the knowledge of God.

COLOSSIANS 1:9–10
NRSV

Just as our outer gardens need water to grow and thrive, our inner gardens need prayer to grow and thrive in wisdom, understanding, and knowledge of God. Our prayers for ourselves are not enough to produce spiritual growth. One kind of flower growing in my garden may be beautiful, but several complementary floral varieties make my garden even more pleasing to the eye.

So it is with prayer and spiritual growth. We need a fellowship of prayer, other Christians committed to praying for our spiritual growth. We grow in the beauty of the Lord because we are rooted in a garden of prayer. Prayer is not a private experience—it is a communal experience. We are lifted up on the fragrance of another's prayers. Our spirits are fed, watered, and nourished by the light of God in answer to the prayers offered in love and compassion by believers.

Likewise, when we offer up prayers for spiritual growth on behalf of another we discover that we grow spiritually as well. Joining in a fellowship of prayer is part of leading worthy lives pleasing to God. We can't help but grow in spiritual wisdom, understanding, and the knowledge of God when we pray for others.

Week 21

Exercise:

Make a mutual commitment with at least one friend to pray for each other's spiritual growth. Focus your prayers for one another on asking that each of you "may be filled with the knowledge of God's will in all spiritual wisdom and understanding, so that you may lead lives worthy of the Lord, fully pleasing to him, as you bear fruit in every good work and as you grow in the knowledge of God." Of course, you will want to pray for other aspects of each other's lives as well, but make a special commitment to pray for one another's spiritual growth.

If possible, agree to meet regularly in your gardens this summer, where living things grow and thrive all around you. Gardens make wonderful places for prayer. Discuss how you have prayed for one another and share any experiences of spiritual growth you've had. End your time of sharing with a brief prayer.

If you are already in a prayer partnership that includes prayers for spiritual growth, consider meeting with that partner in your garden.

In the Outer Garden section, jot down your prayer for spiritual growth on behalf of your prayer partner. In the Inner Garden section, record your own experiences of spiritual growth as a result of your partner's prayers.

Lord Jesus, as I enter a garden of prayer, give me discernment to pray well for the spiritual growth of another. May you be pleased to answer prayers others offer for my growth in you. Strengthen me to be a ceaseless worker in this garden of prayer that we all might lead lives worthy of you. In your name. Amen.

Outer Garden

Inner Garden

Like palm-groves that
stretch far away,
like gardens beside a
river,
like aloes that the LORD
has planted,
like cedar trees beside the
waters.

NUMBERS 24:6 NRSV

This verse is part of a blessing on the people of Israel. Balak, king of Moab, watched as Israel swarmed out of the wilderness to conquer nation after nation. Alarmed by how numerous Israel was, Balak sent for Balaam to curse Israel so that Balak might defeat them in battle. But Balaam acted on God's command instead of Balak's and blessed the people of Israel. Balaam's blessing compared Israel to groves and gardens that spread over the land and took root in it.

God's blessing is powerful. Words uttered in blessing are like living things, like seeds that take root in the one who is blessed. When the word of God comes to us through a blessing, it empowers us to do God's will. And when we receive God's blessing, we experience the love of God and are made special by his blessing.

Our gardens are places where we receive God's blessing. Ever since the Spirit of God moved over Eden and pronounced it good, that original blessing continues to reach each of us through our gardens. They nurture us, restore us, and empower us so that we may go back into the world to seek and work for the will of God.

Week 22

Exercise:

As you work or rest in your garden this week, open yourself to experiencing God's blessing there. Pay attention to the ways God may be blessing you through your garden. Record in the Outer Garden section the ways God has blessed you.

Also reflect on how you have experienced God's blessings in other ways. Ask yourself:

- How has God blessed me through the church?

- How have I received God's blessing through an individual?

- In what other ways has God's blessing come to me?

- How have these blessings empowered me to seek and do God's will?

Record your answers in the Inner Garden section.

Lord, I thank you for the many ways you bless me now. Let me be ever attentive to the blessings you send. Let me always return thanks for your blessings. And, as I receive your blessings into my heart, guide me always to seek and do your will. In the name of Jesus Christ. Amen.

Outer Garden

Inner Garden

Summer

And I have called for a drought on the land and the hills, on the grain, the new wine, the oil, on what the soil produces, on human beings and animals, and on all their labors.

HAGGAI 1:11 NRSV

Many gardeners have experienced drought. The price of water goes up; its use becomes restricted; drought-resistant plants replace dying, water-loving ones; the heat turns gardening into a chore. When drought affects farming, food prices go up. And in many countries, a serious drought brings the threat of famine. No doubt about it—drought can be a serious hardship.

Many of us have also experienced serious spiritual drought at some time in our lives. Our prayer lives dry up; our love for spiritual things fades like a delicate plant exposed to the desert sun; and God seems far away, leaving our spirits scorched. Spiritual droughts can happen naturally to anyone intent on living the Christian life.

Julian of Norwich, a thirteenth-century English mystic, advised those suffering spiritual drought to "pray inwardly, even if you do not enjoy it. It does good, though you feel nothing. Yes, even though you think you are doing nothing."† When we continue to seek after God, even though we don't feel anything or we feel that God is far away, the simple act of prayer is like water to our parched souls.

---

†*Revelations of Divine Love*, 1373.

Week 23

Exercise:

Julian's advice is good for times of spiritual drought. We must continue to pray though we may feel nothing. God is not far away but is as near as our next breath. Simple prayers are like gentle rain in the desert—slowly they refresh our souls. In the Inner Garden section, write a short, simple prayer to pray during times of spiritual dryness.

Add a drought-resistant plant to your garden as a reminder to you during times of natural or spiritual drought that God sustains life always. Record in the Outer Garden section the kind of drought-resistant plant you selected and where you put it in your garden.

Holy Spirit, you walk alongside me, even during times of spiritual dryness. O Lord, though I do not feel your presence, I trust that I am ever in your sight. In Jesus' name. Amen. ❧

Outer Garden

Inner Garden

Summer

I am the vine, you are the branches. Those who abide in me and I in them bear much fruit, because apart from me you can do nothing.

JOHN 15:5 NRSV

Any gardener who raises fruit-bearing trees knows that the bud, the blossom, and finally the fruit comes from the strength of the tree itself. The tree gathers energy from sunlight and water and nutrients from the soil; it attracts birds and insects for pollination—all for the production of fruit.

The same sort of process exists in our relationship with the Lord. Jesus' relationship with us is so close, so intimate, that we live inside each other. We are "powered," as it were, by Jesus living in us *and* by our living in Jesus. Like a vine and its branches, there could be no fruit without both. Jesus gives us all we need to produce fruit in our lives, which in turn gives glory to God. Jesus the vine supplies us with all we need, even his very self, to enjoy, love, and live in God.

Week 24

Exercise:

Set aside some time this week to sit in your garden and meditate on the fruit-bearing or flower-bearing plants. Think about how the fruit or flowers got to be there:

🌿 What went into making the fruit and flowers?

🌿 How do the flowers or fruit interact with the tree, vine, or plant?

Record your answers in as much detail as possible in the Outer Garden section.

As you continue to sit in your garden, meditate on Jesus living in you and you living in Jesus.

🌿 How does Jesus abiding in you and you abiding in him make you feel?

🌿 How is this extremely intimate relationship bearing fruit for God in your life?

Record your answers in the Inner Garden section.

Lord, you are all my strength for living a life that pleases you. Give me the grace to experience you living inside me every moment of every day. By your mercy, let me live and move and have my being in you. May the fruit our relationship produces honor and glorify you and give me joy. In Christ's name. Amen. 🌿

Outer Garden

_____

_____

_____

_____

_____

_____

_____

_____

_____

Inner Garden

_____

_____

_____

_____

_____

_____

_____

_____

Summer

In the morning sow your seed, and at evening do not let your hands be idle; for you do not know which will prosper, this or that, or whether both alike will be good.

ECCLESIASTES 11:6
NRSV

The writer of Ecclesiastes believed in diversifying his portfolio. Work in your garden in the morning, but keep working at this and that in the evening so that you will prosper just in case either your garden or another thing fails. Ecclesiastes 11:6 is a word about survival to a people whose livelihoods depended on the produce of the land. But we can playfully expand on this verse, applying it not only to our gardens, but to our spiritual lives too.

Summer is a great time to busily play in our gardens, on vacation, or with hobbies or projects. Summer is the season to enjoy God's creation. We are not idle during summer, but we keep busy with holy play.

Exercise:

This week you may want to reevaluate the diversity of plant life in your garden:

- Are the plants and flowers diverse enough to be interesting?

- If you have a vegetable garden, are some things coming along better than others?

- Are there opportunities for creative transplanting or replacing some plants with new ones?

- Where can you tinker in your garden and give it a little freshness?

Make your notes in the Outer Garden section.

If your reevaluation shows you that your garden could use a little something extra, do it. If you're happy with the diversity in your garden, congratulations!

Week 25

Our Inner Gardens can use a little summer diversity too. Take some time this week to reevaluate your prayer life: does it feel a bit dull?

If your answer is yes, try the following this week:

Day 1: Dedicate the day to thanksgiving and gratitude to God for his love and faithfulness.

Day 2: Choose a favorite psalm and pray it over and over again until the psalmist's song becomes your personal prayer.

Day 3: Spend time today in intercessory prayer for people you *don't* know: for example, the homeless, those in war-torn countries, people suffering from hunger. Also give thanks for people you don't know: our government, your local police, other churches' ministries in your neighborhood.

Day 4: Spend time today in intercessory prayer for people you *do* know, and use your imagination. For example, instead of just saying words to God about your children, imagine Jesus holding them in his lap as he smiles and laughs with them.

Day 5: Pray for yourself in your garden, either sitting quietly or as you work. Pray especially for your prayer life—that God would show you many different ways to enjoy God's presence in prayer.

Record your daily experiences in the Inner Garden section.

Lord, let my prayer life reflect the diversity and joy of your creation. Let me never be afraid to play at prayer and try new things. Help me to trust that you will guide me to prayer that pleases you. In the name of Jesus Christ. Amen.

Outer Garden

_____

_____

_____

_____

_____

_____

_____

_____

Inner Garden

_____

_____

_____

_____

_____

_____

_____

_____

Summer

God gave Solomon very great wisdom, discernment, and breadth of understanding as vast as the sand on the seashore, so that Solomon's wisdom surpassed the wisdom of all the people of the east, and all the wisdom of Egypt. . . . He would speak of trees, from the cedar that is in the Lebanon to the hyssop that grows in the wall.

1 KINGS 4:29–30, 33*a*
NRSV

King Solomon's many accomplishments included being a naturalist and a master gardener. His wisdom was great in part because it included an understanding of growing things. And the psalms are full of wise comparisons of grasses, plants, and flowers to human beings.

A friend of mine is a professional naturalist. He has spent his life observing and learning the ways of nature. But what gives him most joy and makes him most wise about the natural world is his beautiful, elaborate garden. He carefully cultivates rare native wildflowers as well as other flowers and plants. And he is one of the wisest men I've known. His acute observations and insights into human behavior often stem from his reflections and observations of the way his garden grows.

Week 26

Exercise:

Our gardens can contribute to our wisdom too. Observe your garden in detail this week. Write in the Outer Garden section anything that strikes you about its beauty, what's blooming, your struggles with weeds or pests, and so on. You may want to select one plant or flower for your intense observation.

Let your garden make you a little wiser about yourself or others this week. As you observe your garden, record in the Inner Garden section what it teaches you. For example: I observe my climbing jasmine daily sends out new vines and is beginning to wrap itself around a lavender bush—I know I will have to prune the jasmine soon for the sake of the lavender. God likewise prunes in us that which clings too much to people or things so we don't overpower them.

Jesus, you are the Great Teacher. You make me wise about your way. You use Scripture, church, and even my garden to help me know you better. Increase my wisdom this week as I seek you in my garden. In your Name. Amen. ✣

Outer Garden

_____

_____

_____

_____

_____

_____

_____

Inner Garden

_____

_____

_____

_____

_____

_____

_____

*S*ummer

Now there was a garden in the place where he was crucified, and in the garden there was a new tomb in which no one had ever been laid.

JOHN 19:41 NRSV

John's Gospel tells us not once, but twice, that there was a garden in which Christ was crucified and buried. The significance of this was not lost on the early church. Jesus' crucifixion, burial, and later resurrection in a garden was symbolic of a new Eden, a new creation. Just as the original Eden was lost forever because of our sinfulness, Eden is now restored through Christ's taking upon himself the sins of the world.

In gardens new creation begins. Every gardener knows that death must take place in the garden so that new growth can happen. Pruning, weeding, uprooting diseased plants, even removing pests make our gardens healthier, more beautiful places.

And so it is with God, the greatest Gardener of all. We are God's garden. In a manner of speaking, the Lord prunes and weeds the souls of his people so that we may more fully become his new creatures. We participate in Jesus' crucifixion when we die daily to sin; and we rise daily as new creations in Christ. The work God began in the original Eden climaxed in the new Eden and continues in us, the people of God.

Week 27

Exercise:

Set aside time this week to weed, prune, or thin out your garden. Record in the Outer Garden section the work you did and how you see that work contributing to the health and beauty of your garden. Also record where your garden still needs this kind of work.

If you have an indoor garden, where weeding or pruning may not apply, visit a public garden sometime this week and watch the gardeners at work there. Better yet, talk to them and ask how their work shapes the garden to make it more beautiful.

As you work to weed or thin out your garden, reflect on the following questions:

- How is God at work in my life pulling up weeds or pruning back dead branches?

- What is God allowing to die in my life so that Christ may live?

Later, record your reflections in the Inner Garden section.

O Lord, you are the Great Gardener. Do unto me according to your will. Weed out and crucify the sin in my life so that I may live with Christ. Amen.

Outer Garden

_____

_____

_____

_____

_____

_____

_____

_____

Inner Garden

_____

_____

_____

_____

_____

_____

_____

Summer

All gardens are living reminders of hope. When we plant a garden, we make real our hope that life will flourish and thrive. It is no accident that God created us in a garden, Eden, his promise that life would begin and continue in the midst of a world made of seas and dry land. In the garden, God nurtured and loved his creatures. He graced it by his very presence, walking in the cool of the day.

When we plant a garden we imitate God—we bring a little bit of Eden into our lives. Our gardens may be pleasing to the eye or used as sources of food, both beautiful and useful at once. Our gardens nourish our souls with the beauty of God's creation and our bodies with sustenance from the bounty of the Lord.

Exercise:

In the Outer Garden section, make a list of all the ways your garden nourishes, refreshes, and restores you. For example, at the end of the week your list may look something like this:

1. My garden provides me and my family with vegetables I can store for winter.
2. My garden is full of color—looking at it gives me energy and hope.
3. My garden is a cool place on a hot day.
4. My garden gives me flowers for the table, making mealtimes special.

Week 28

Then make a list in the Inner Garden section of how your spirit is nourished, refreshed, and restored by God. Include in this list how God has nourished you through your garden and how God nourishes you through family, friends, and activities. For example, at the end of the week your list may look something like this:

1. God nourishes my inner garden when I work in my outer garden.
2. God nourishes my inner garden when I share a cup of coffee with Susan.
3. God nourishes my inner garden when I cook for my family.
4. God nourishes my inner garden when I quietly wait on the presence of God in my outer garden.

Don't limit yourself to any number of items—the above lists are samples only. List as many as you can throughout the week.

Once you have completed this exercise, return to these lists whenever you are feeling spiritually or physically depleted. Rereading and practicing the things you listed will help nourish your spirit.

Lord, in your presence is refreshment, nourishment, and healing. Show me how to find you this week in my garden and in my spirit and in my relationships. I give you thanks, O God, for the many ways you restore my soul. Give me the wisdom now and in the future to take the time to seek your presence in all aspects of my life. I pray in the name of Jesus Christ. Amen. ❧

Outer Garden

_____
_____
_____
_____
_____
_____
_____
_____
_____
_____

Inner Garden

_____
_____
_____
_____
_____
_____
_____
_____
_____

 Summer

From the bed where it
was planted
it was transplanted
to good soil by abundant
waters,
so that it might produce
branches
and bear fruit
and become a noble vine.

EZEKIEL 17:7*b*–8 NRSV

Since I have a container garden, I do a lot of transplanting. As small plants grow into large bushes I repot them into bigger pots or plant them in my landlord's garden. Transplanting is a change for the better in the long run; it will help the plant continue to grow and thrive. But the immediate result of transplanting can be root shock. To lessen the shock of being uprooted and replanted, I use fertilizers and various other treatments.

Transplanting is a kind of managed change in our gardens. I have a friend who used to tell me that "all change, even change for the better, is experienced as loss." Anyone who has ever had her life uprooted by the arrival of her first child knows how true my friend's words are. A new baby is definitely change for the better. But a woman who finds herself transplanted into a different lifestyle, that of being a mother, can suffer a little "root shock." With the joy may also come feelings of loss, of longing for the old days when she had time to herself.

God manages change in our lives. He sometimes transplants us to a different place so we may thrive and grow. But change, leaving something or someone familiar behind for a new place or new relationships, can be hard—and we may experience a little root shock.

Week 29

Exercise:

The next time you are moving plants around in your garden, pay extra attention to what you are doing—especially to prevent root shock. For example, you may give the plant extra water or fertilizer or prepare a special mulch. Pay attention to how you nurture your plant through the shock of being uprooted. In the Outer Garden section, record your actions in as much detail as possible. Also record any feelings you experienced while transplanting.

Praying and taking good care of ourselves are the best antidotes to root shock. If your life is undergoing significant change in some way, briefly record your experience in the Inner Garden section. Then draft a plan of how you will take care of yourself during this experience of being "transplanted." Finally, write a special prayer you can pray during this time of transition.

Lord, I trust you to manage the many changes in my life. But change can be hard, and I need you, Lord, to strengthen me so that I may take root in a new place filled with hidden blessings and promises. In your name. Amen. ❧

Outer Garden

Inner Garden

Autumn

Autumn

And they found it written in the law, which the LORD had commanded by Moses, that the people of Israel should live in booths during the festival of the seventh month, and that they should publish and proclaim in all their towns and in Jerusalem as follows, "Go out to the hills and bring branches of olive, wild olive, myrtle, palm, and other leafy trees to make booths, as it is written."

NEHEMIAH 8:14–15
NRSV

The law of God commanded Israel to build booths made of "leafy trees" during the annual harvest festival. These booths were to commemorate the Lord's protection of Israel during their wanderings in the desert. Nehemiah wrote to the generation of Israel that had recently returned from captivity in Babylon. God's people were rediscovering the law of the Lord as commanded by Moses. And they easily identified with the earlier generation's forty years in the desert. With a special poignancy, Nehemiah's generation was to construct harvest booths in honor of God's protection when they were in captivity.

As gardeners, especially those of us who grow fruits and vegetables, we understand harvest time. We know the joy of gathering flowers and produce as they become ready for picking in the fall. With our gardens' bounty in our arms, it's easy to breathe a prayer of thanks to God. Nehemiah reminds us that harvest time is also a time to commemorate God's protection. We remember and celebrate how the Lord feeds and shelters us—especially when we have experienced dark or difficult times.

Week 30

Exercise:

It may not be possible to build booths this autumn, but we can celebrate and remember the many ways God has protected us this past year. As you harvest fruit, vegetables, or flowers this week, set some aside. Record in the Outer Garden section what you harvested this year.

With what you've set aside, make a special flower arrangement or display of fruit or vegetables. In the Inner Garden section, list all the ways you've experienced God's protection this year. Select a dozen items from your list and write them on autumnal-colored construction paper (you may wish to use several different colors). Cut out each of the items, fold each in half, and place them attractively among the flowers or produce. Then offer up a prayer of thanks to the Lord who has protected you in the past and watches over you now.

Lord, your protection this year has been a great blessing. I give you thanks and praise for the many, many ways you've provided for me, cared for me, and delivered me. May my offering of thanks and praise be pleasing to you. In the name of Jesus. Amen. ❧

Outer Garden

_____

_____

_____

_____

_____

_____

_____

_____

Inner Garden

_____

_____

_____

_____

_____

_____

_____

_____

_____

Autumn

My Father is glorified by this, that you bear much fruit and become my disciples.

JOHN 15:8 NRSV

The life of discipleship, our bearing fruit as Jesus' disciples, glorifies the Father. The disciple's life is disciplined, but not in a negative way that promises punishment or fear. The disciplined life gently cultivates the fruits of the Spirit through prayer, love for both friends and enemies, hospitality, service to the community, worship, Bible study, and reflection.

Our gardens teach us about such a life. Gardening is a discipline that we gladly accept. As gardeners we practice the discipline of watering, seasonal planting, feeding and fertilizing, working to improve the soil, weeding, pruning, and harvesting. If our gardens are to grow and become beautiful, we must take care of them.

If we are to grow into the image of Christ and glorify the Father, we must also take care of ourselves and one another.

Week 31

Exercise:

In the Outer Garden section, record the disciplines you practiced in your garden this week. Also write about how it feels to practice these disciplines—which ones are more pleasant than others? What makes some of the less pleasant gardening disciplines difficult to perform?

Cultivate your inner garden by selecting a spiritual discipline to practice throughout the week—for example, prayer, love, service, worship, hospitality, or Bible study. As you go through the week, pay attention to the impact your chosen discipline has on your life, the lives of others, and your relationship with God. Record your experience in the Inner Garden section.

Father, let me glorify you this week. Cultivate in me the fruit of your Spirit through spiritual disciplines that bring me the joy of your presence. I am your disciple, O Lord, and all I have, all I am, is yours. In Christ's name. Amen.

Outer Garden

_____
_____
_____
_____
_____
_____
_____
_____
_____

Inner Garden

_____
_____
_____
_____
_____
_____
_____
_____
_____
_____

Autumn

He also said, "The kingdom of God is as if someone would scatter seed on the ground, and would sleep and rise night and day, and the seed would sprout and grow, he does not know how."

MARK 4:26–27 NRSV

I have been gardening for some time now, but unlike "Mary, Mary, Quite Contrary," I cannot tell you *how* my garden grows. I plant it, I water and fertilize it, and I weed it—I provide the *conditions* for growth. But exactly how growth happens remains a mystery to me. My garden grows because it is God's good will that it grow.

The growth of the kingdom of God—God's rule, establishing a place of justice and grace on earth—is also a mystery, known only to the Father. Even Jesus couldn't fully explain it to us humans.

All we can do is provide the *conditions* for growth of the kingdom of God: to love and forgive through the grace extended to us by God, to treat kindly the stranger in our midst, to feed those who are hungry, to share with those in pain our hope in the gospel of Jesus Christ. It is God's business to grow his kingdom. We are God's gardeners, nurturing, tending, and caring for the kingdom as best we can.

Week 32

Exercise:

Go out to your garden and make yourself comfortable. In the Outer Garden section, list all the conditions you provide for your garden's growth.

Then sit quietly for a while and reflect on what conditions you provide for the growth of God's kingdom. List those in the Inner Garden section. Be as specific as possible (loving a difficult neighbor, forgiving a spouse, ministering to shut-ins). Next write a brief paragraph describing what God's kingdom looks like to you. Or, if you prefer not to write, sketch a picture of the kingdom of God as you see it.

Lord, help me to be faithful, encouraging the growth of your kingdom around me. Give me the wisdom and strength I need to offer the hope of your gospel to those in need or pain. I thank you for glimpses of your kingdom as I go about my day. In your name. Amen.

Outer Garden

_____
_____
_____
_____
_____
_____
_____
_____

Inner Garden

_____
_____
_____
_____
_____
_____
_____
_____

Autumn

God said, "See, I have given you every plant yielding seed that is upon the face of all the earth, and every tree with seed in its fruit; you shall have them for food. And to every beast of the earth, and to every bird of the air, and to everything that creeps on the earth, everything that has the breath of life, I have given every green plant for food." And it was so.

GENESIS 1:29–30 NRSV

Our gardens teach us that we are stewards, caretakers of God's creation. We cannot make a flower bloom or a tree grow. We can only work to make the conditions right for growth. And sometimes we can't even do that—sometimes the weather is too hot or too cold, too dry or too wet.

Our gardens are gifts from God that teach us that all life, all growth is in his hands. Only God has the power to create and sustain life. All life seems more precious because of the care we lavish on our gardens. Taking care of them extends our appreciation for other living things. God made us stewards over his creation so that we could rejoice in it, admire it, and love it as much as God does. And we never take for granted a single bloom, a ripe tomato, or the red leaves of a maple tree.

Week 33

Exercise:

Go into your garden and pick a blossom, vegetable, or distinctive leaf. Float the blossom in a bowl, or put the vegetable or leaf in a special dish. In the Outer Garden section, draw a picture of your choice. If you prefer not to draw, use words to describe it in as much detail as possible.

Use the blossom, vegetable, or leaf as the focus of your prayer time this week. In your Inner Garden section, write a praise prayer inspired by the fruit of your garden. Remember: Don't take the produce of your garden for granted. Let your garden inspire you to praise and honor your Creator.

Lord God, you are the Creator, Redeemer, and Sustainer of all life. Remind me every day that all life is precious. In your mercy, protect me from taking life for granted that I may ever sing your praises to the glory of your name. Amen.

Outer Garden

_____
_____
_____
_____
_____
_____
_____
_____

Inner Garden

_____
_____
_____
_____
_____
_____
_____
_____

Autumn

He said to them, "The harvest is plentiful, but the laborers are few; therefore ask the Lord of the harvest to send out laborers into his harvest."

LUKE 10:2 NRSV

My favorite season of the year is autumn. Autumn in California is brief and very subtle: fall arrives with a slight change in the angle of sunlight, and all the leaves suddenly turn brown and drop off the trees. I've always dreamed of spending an autumn in New England or the northern mid-west where autumn lingers, the leaves change to gold and crimson, the evening air has a bite to it, and frost covers the pumpkins.

Harvesttime, though, is a part of California's autumn, especially in northern California's wine country. During October the grapes are harvested for wine. The vineyards are full of workers harvesting the grapes, and the winery presses work to full capacity creating a feeling of excitement and anticipation, especially if the weather has been exceptionally good for the vines.

Our Lord asks us to join in the harvest. As we harvest the fruit and flowers from our gardens, we also harvest friends and family for the love of God.

Week 34

Exercise:

As you harvest your garden this fall, let each vegetable, fruit, or flower symbolize a friend or family member you are bringing into the kingdom. Pay attention to how you feel as you bring in your harvest for the day. Record your thoughts and feelings in the Outer Garden section.

Plan a special supper from the produce of your garden. If your garden only produces flowers or herbs, make a special harvest arrangement to decorate the supper table. Invite several friends to dinner. Share the gospel with them by the way you return thanks to God for the fruit of his creation. Or begin the evening with a short Scripture passage. Briefly tell those gathered the purpose of the supper—to glorify God and to give thanks for how he provides for each one present. Record the events of the evening in your Inner Garden section.

Lord of the harvest, you bless us with the joy of gardening and the pleasure of harvesting from your creation. I thank you now, O Lord, for friends and family who know you and friends and family who don't. Make me a laborer in your harvest by showing your love through me. In Jesus' name. Amen.

139

Outer Garden

_____
_____
_____
_____
_____
_____
_____
_____
_____

Inner Garden

_____
_____
_____
_____
_____
_____
_____
_____
_____

Autumn

It should come as no surprise that where we sow the best of our time and talent we stand the best chance of reaping the rewards of our labor. We gardeners know that only by putting in time and energy do we produce beautiful, bountiful gardens.

The proverb also points us to a truth beyond our gardens: to stay away from worthless pursuits. When we give the best of ourselves to our family and friends, our work, and our church, we are faithful stewards of the blessings God has given us. At times the hard work involved in "tilling" our lives produces beauty and bounty in our relationships. Occasionally, no matter how faithful we have been investing our time and energy in what is important, the harvest seems smaller than we anticipated. Still, any other way of life makes "no sense"— it is the life of a fool. If we continue to tend and nurture our relationships, the work God has given us to do, our lives, our gardens, will be bountiful in this world and the next.

Week 35

Exercise:

In your Outer Garden section, record how much time and energy you put into your garden this week. What do you expect as a result of tending it? In the Inner Garden section, compare your life, work, and relationships to the garden you tend and nurture. Where is your time and energy going now? Are you happy with how you are investing in your life? Or are there areas that are distracted by "worthless pursuits"?

Lord God, give me the energy and strength to invest my life in ways that are pleasing to you. Give me the wisdom to turn away from worthless pursuits so that I may enjoy your will. In Jesus' name. Amen.

Outer Garden

_____
_____
_____
_____
_____
_____
_____
_____

Inner Garden

_____
_____
_____
_____
_____
_____
_____
_____
_____

Autumn

You did not choose me but I chose you. And I appointed you to go and bear fruit, fruit that will last, so that the Father will give you whatever you ask him in my name.

JOHN 15:16 NRSV

We are Jesus' chosen people. Jesus chose us to bear "fruit that will last." Unlike that which grows in our gardens, the sort of fruit Jesus spoke about won't spoil. What we bear in our lives here on earth is the everlasting fruit of the kingdom: loving and forgiving one another, worshiping God, seeking after the Lord with all our hearts, caring for those weaker and poorer than ourselves. It is eternal fruit that testifies to our citizenship in the kingdom of God.

Jesus also told us that because we bear this everlasting fruit, the Father will give us whatever we ask in Jesus' name so that his kingdom may be glorified throughout the world. Like the fruit we bear, answered prayers also testify to the world of our citizenship in his kingdom.

I like to think of my garden as a little portion of God's kingdom made visible. I can see the fruit of my work there: fragrant herbs that please the senses, making my garden a beautiful place. My outer garden reflects my inner garden—the "fruit that will last," and the work and fruit of my prayers show the world a little portion of the kingdom of God.

Week 36

Exercise:

In the Outer Garden section, answer the following question: How does my garden give me a glimpse of the kingdom of God? Be as detailed and specific as possible.

For example, you may write, "My roses are beautiful and beauty is always a sign of God's kingdom. God is at work in my roses as he is in all of his creation." Or, "My garden is the fruit of a lot of hard work. I love the work I do in my garden because I know I am working with God to create a place of peace and beauty in the world."

In the Inner Garden section, make a "fruitful" prayer list. Be courageous in asking the Father what you want him to give you. Feel free to expand this list and return to it throughout the year, noting answered prayers and how those prayers glorified God's kingdom.

Lord Jesus, guide me in my prayers to the Father. Let the prayers I pray and the fruit I bear show a little bit of your kingdom to the world. May my inner and outer life proclaim your goodness and love to me and all you have made. In your name. Amen.

Outer Garden

_____
_____
_____
_____
_____
_____
_____
_____

Inner Garden

_____
_____
_____
_____
_____
_____
_____
_____
_____

Autumn

That fiftieth year shall be a jubilee for you: you shall not sow, or reap the aftergrowth, or harvest the unpruned vines.

LEVITICUS 25:11 NRSV

Sometimes I avoid reading Leviticus because of all the dry and, well, somewhat boring laws laid out for the people of God. Too often I forget that the laws, commandments, and regulations of Leviticus were given to Israel so that they could love and even *enjoy* God better.

Such a law is that regarding the jubilee year. Every fifty years God's people celebrated and enjoyed the providence of the land, which was God's gift to them. Jubilee included celebrating God by cancelling all debts, redistributing land to make sure everybody had enough land to live on, and freeing slaves and indentured servants. In return, the Lord provided his people with enough to eat so they could enjoy the land.

How sad for us that the church, so much attached to the modern world, has lost the commandment of jubilee! We must use our imaginations and find ways to keep jubilee and enjoy the living God and the land he gave to us.

Exercise:

This week, plan a jubilee for yourself and your family. Include time to cancel financial and spiritual debts between one another. Have an honest discussion with your family about the joy of forgiving each other and cancelling debts to give glory to God. Close your time together by praying the Lord's Prayer.

Week 37

You have no slaves to free, but take some time to reflect on how you may have subtly enslaved yourself or those you love. For example, you may discover you have made a slave of yourself with an overwhelming need for emotional or financial security. Or you may discover you have such high expectations of your children that they have little room to become simply who God made them. Once you find how you have enslaved yourself or those you love, proclaim a day of liberty. Write down what enslaves you or your family and burn the piece of paper. Spend some time in prayer releasing yourself and those you love into God's loving care; ask God to honor your proclamation of liberty by giving you the strength you need to live freely in him.

Finally, include a day celebrating God in your garden. Have a barbecue or party for friends. Tell them that it is a jubilee party to celebrate the love of God, your relationships, and the land in which your beautiful garden grows.

Use the Inner Garden and Outer Garden sections to plan your jubilee.

Almighty God, may our time of jubilee celebrate and glorify you. Guide each of us so that we may enjoy you better. Bless this time so that we can become the people you have created us to be, in the glory of your name. Amen. ❧

Outer Garden

_____

_____

_____

_____

_____

_____

_____

_____

Inner Garden

_____

_____

_____

_____

_____

_____

_____

_____

Autumn

For everything there is a season, and a time for every matter under heaven:

a time to be born, and a time to die;

a time to plant, and a time to pluck up what is planted.

ECCLESIASTES 3:1–2
NRSV

Gardeners live seasonally. We have learned the best time to plant and the best time to harvest. Our gardens teach us that there is a time for everything—and that things change. Bad times may happen, but good times will return.

I once interviewed for what I considered my "dream job." The interview was intense and the process by which the employer reached a decision was long and drawn out. Then came the nerve-wracking wait to hear the results. Finally, I learned that another candidate had been chosen instead of me. I felt devastated for several days. My emotional turning point came when friends from out of town sent a gift of a beautiful blue hydrangea plant. A simple message was attached: "Don't lose heart!" I joyfully planted the hydrangea in a big redwood tub. With the support and love of friends such as these, I began to see that the job wasn't as important as I had imagined. My perspective and my feelings began to change.

Don't lose heart. Things change. God has made each of us able to change with the seasons—to rejoice during the good times and to weep during the bad times. The fellowship of God's people and the love of God will see us through.

Week 38

Exercise:

Perhaps you know someone who is going through a rough time this week. Go into your garden and harvest some flowers or vegetables to give that person as a present. Deliver them with a word of encouragement or a prayer. Describe your gift in the Outer Garden section.

In the Inner Garden section identify the current "season" of your life (autumn, winter, spring, or summer). Describe how this season feels to you now—is it a time of contentment or dissatisfaction, a time of renewal and faith, or a time of questioning and doubt? How do you see the season of your life changing the person you are becoming? How is God directing this season of your life?

Almighty God, you are the Lord of time. I am in your hands. Take me and mold me into the image of your Christ. Let this season of my life be a time of transformation and growth in your Spirit. Be with me, O Lord, in good times and bad so that in whatever circumstance I find myself I may give you praise and honor. In Jesus' name. Amen.

Outer Garden

_____
_____
_____
_____
_____
_____
_____
_____
_____

Inner Garden

_____
_____
_____
_____
_____
_____
_____
_____
_____

Autumn

"Waste not, want not"; so the saying goes. It is now generally fashionable to recycle as much as we can. Many gardeners already experience the joy of composting—turning unwanted vegetable matter into nutrient-rich mulch for their gardens. But these are not merely popular, fashionable things to do. They are also signs of good stewardship of God's creation. Yet in our rush to use up everything, we must remember it is also good stewardship to leave a little for those not as fortunate as ourselves.

Leviticus 23:22 presents a wonderful stewardship passage. God reminds his people to leave a bit of their harvest for the poor. We need to balance our recycling and composting efforts with leaving enough for the poor and immigrants among us. During this harvest season, we can offer the "gleanings" to others with thanks to God.

Week 39

Exercise:

As you harvest, set aside a portion for the "poor and alien." Should your harvest consist of fruit and vegetables, donate some to a local soup kitchen. If you harvest flowers from your garden, donate bouquets to a local nursing home or hospital for people without friends or family to visit them.

You may want to make Thanksgiving even more special this year by including a family who faces financial difficulties. Perhaps your church supports refugees or an immigrant family. Find out how you can help make Thanksgiving a time for them to be able to give thanks.

Record in your Outer Garden section the portion of your harvest you set aside to share with others and who you donated it to. In your Inner Garden section write about how you felt when you shared Thanksgiving or harvest with others.

I give you thanks, O Lord, for the extra bounty. Help me to balance my efforts of finding renewed uses for your creation with giving enough to others who need help. Make me a worthy steward, O God, so that on the last day we can greet each other with joy. In Christ's name. Amen. ❧

Outer Garden

_____
_____
_____
_____
_____
_____
_____
_____

Inner Garden

_____
_____
_____
_____
_____
_____
_____
_____

Autumn

Haggai the prophet communicated God's displeasure with the people of Israel because, after being released from captivity in Babylon, they built new homes for themselves before they built a house for the Lord. The issue was much more than merely building a place for God—the real issue was the proper worship of God before all else. As a result of the people's neglect, God brought a drought upon the land to ruin their gardens and produce. But once the people built a house for the Lord, God reversed the curse by promising to bless them.

We were created to worship God, and all life flows from our worship. Our gardens are no exception; they are holy places. Like everything else in our lives, they have their source in our worship of God and our desire to please him. Our gardens reflect a little bit of the original Eden. We cannot help but be inspired to praise and worship God for their beauty and abundance.

Week 40

Exercise:

If you belong to a Bible study, circle, or prayer group, invite members to an informal worship service in your garden. Autumn is the perfect season for a service that praises and thanks God for all of creation and the bounty of your garden. In the Outer Garden section, outline a simple service, which may consist of hymns, prayers, a reading of Scripture, and a brief exhortation on the text. Ask members of your group to perform various aspects of the worship service.

After the worship service is over, record your experience in the Inner Garden section. Note the impact the service had on the others, as well as on your own heart.

Lord God Almighty, you are worthy at all times to be praised. Bless this service of worship in my garden. Let all who enter know they tread on holy ground, because you, O Lord, are the source of all creation. In Jesus' name. Amen.

Outer Garden

_____

_____

_____

_____

_____

_____

_____

_____

_____

Inner Garden

_____

_____

_____

_____

_____

_____

_____

_____

Autumn

Six years you shall sow your field, and six years you shall prune your vineyard, and gather in their yield; but in the seventh year there shall be a sabbath of complete rest for the land, a sabbath for the LORD: you shall not sow your field or prune your vineyard.

LEVITICUS 25:3–4 NRSV

God's people were commanded to keep the sabbath, not only the seventh day of the week, but every seventh year as well. This sabbath year was a year of complete rest for the land. Israel knew that they did not own the land—God gave them the land to use. In fact, Israel knew they belonged to the land as they belonged to God. This is why Israel called the land on which they grew their crops, vineyards, and gardens sacred. The Sabbath year reinforced the fact that the land belonged to God.

Likewise, we do not own the land in which we grow our gardens. The earth and all that is in it belongs to God. We, too, belong to the land because we belong to God, who gives it to us in stewardship. Unlike ancient Israel, we don't keep the sabbath year. But we experience the sabbath every week, usually by attending church services. After church I often spend time working in my garden and doing a few chores around the house to get ready for the coming week. It is hardly a day of "complete rest" for me or my garden. Yet keeping a sabbath, a day of complete rest for our gardens and ourselves, reminds us that we belong wholly to God and so do our gardens. It is an outward sign of our trust in God who is our Creator.

Week 41

Exercise:

Plan to keep next Sunday as a day of sabbath, a day of "complete rest" for you and your garden. This may not be easy—our families demand much from us, and time is precious. But it is possible with a little planning. Tell your family ahead of time what you plan to do and invite them to join you. Then, throughout the week, work a little ahead every day until there are no chores to do either in the house or garden. For example, one weekday I cooked extra food so that on Sunday all I needed to do was reheat lunch and dinner in the microwave. I spent a late afternoon on another weekday doing some extra repotting and pruning on the deck. Use the Outer Garden section to list all the tasks you have to do during the week in order to make Sunday a complete day of rest.

Spend Sunday in your garden—not working in it, but enjoying it as part of God's creation. You may want to bring along this book or your Bible for reading or study. Spend some time throughout the day in prayer. Meditate for a while on the fact that the garden in which you sit is God's creation. But above all relax in the Lord; rest as completely as you can. Enjoy the beauty of your garden—it is a small reflection of Eden. You may want to invite family and friends to join you there, maybe have a picnic of food you prepared earlier in the week. At the end of the day, record in the Inner Garden section your experience of the day.

Lord of the Sabbath, in you I can rest completely. You created your people to worship and enjoy you. You have given me this garden as a place of rest as well as work. To you, O Creator, belongs all thanks and praise. Amen.

Outer Garden

_____
_____
_____
_____
_____
_____
_____
_____
_____

Inner Garden

_____
_____
_____
_____
_____
_____
_____
_____

Winter

Winter

*They shall not build and
another inhabit;
they shall not plant and
another eat;
for like the days of a tree
shall the days of my
people be,
and my chosen shall long
enjoy the work of their
hands.*

ISAIAH 65:22 NRSV

Isaiah communicated God's comforting message to his people during a wintry time. Much of Israel had been carried into captivity by the Babylonian empire. They longed to be free and home again. God's promise that "like the days of a tree shall the days of my people be" offers the comforting image of a strong, ancient tree firmly rooted, unmovable in its native soil. "They shall not build and another inhabit; they shall not plant and another eat; . . . my chosen shall long enjoy the work of their hands" must have warmed the hearts of God's people like the summer sun.

We, too, are God's chosen people. God's promises sustain us during the wintry times in our lives or when the weather outside denies us the comfort and pleasure of working in our gardens. As he did to Israel in exile, God promises us that we will once again plant and build under a summer sun and will long enjoy the work of our hands.

Week 42

Exercise:

Collect God's promises in Scripture that you can refer to during those winter times in your life. On a day when the weather is particularly inclement, set aside an hour to browse through your Bible and write down in the Inner Garden section God's promises that are most meaningful to you. Refer to the promises you chose throughout the winter, especially when you or a loved one faces a difficult time.

If you live in a part of the country where the winters are mild, go to your garden and collect rocks or leaves with interesting patterns or pick any flowers that may be in bloom to make a small bouquet. Bring them inside and dedicate them as special reminders of a particular promise God has for you or a loved one.

Lord God, you promise faithfulness, mercy, and grace to your people. I give you thanks for the promises I collected today. In them I see your love and care for me. May they continue to comfort and warm me this winter and whenever I find myself or my loved ones enduring a wintry time. In the name of Christ. Amen.

Outer Garden

_____

_____

_____

_____

_____

_____

_____

_____

Inner Garden

_____

_____

_____

_____

_____

_____

_____

Winter

He carved the walls of the house all around about with carved engravings of cherubim, palm trees, and open flowers, in the inner and outer rooms.

1 KINGS 6:29 NRSV

Solomon did not leave his magnificent gardens outside the palace but brought them indoors by carving flowers, trees, and cherubim on the walls. By including cherubim in his carvings of plant life, Solomon caused heaven and earth to meet in his indoor garden. It represented not only the gardens outside but heavenly gardens as well.

We may not want to carve our walls, but during the winter, we can find other ways to bring our gardens indoors—along with a little heaven. This winter I discovered the joy of cultivating African violets. The various shades of purples and pinks brighten my windowsill against gray skies. House plants, cut flowers attractively arranged in vases, botanical prints, richly flowered bed coverings, even little table-top fountains can make an indoor springtime of the darkest winter.

Week 43

Exercise:

Practice a little of the wisdom of Solomon. In the Outer Garden section make a list of as many ways as you can to bring your garden indoors for the winter. Then go back over your list and select two or three things you can do to create a little springtime inside.

In your Inner Garden section record how bringing a little of your garden indoors may help lift your winter doldrums. Consider how this will affect your prayer and Bible study.

Jesus, you brighten even my darkest days. Help me to create a garden indoors that I may glory in your creation even during winter. You shall be a lamp to my feet during even the darkest winter days. In your name. Amen. ❧

Outer Garden

_____
_____
_____
_____
_____
_____
_____
_____
_____

Inner Garden

_____
_____
_____
_____
_____
_____
_____
_____

Winter

For the LORD will comfort
Zion;
he will comfort all her
waste places,
and will make her
wilderness like Eden,
her desert like the garden
of the LORD;
joy and gladness will be
found in her,
thanksgiving and the
voice of song.

ISAIAH 51:3 NRSV

I began my own garden when I was unemployed. During that time I needed comfort; my uncertain future seemed to me like one of the "waste places" in Scripture. But when I transplanted my first tiny lavender plant, something inside me felt deeply comforted. It was as though God had touched me through that little plant, making a small oasis in the wilderness I felt inside. Needless to say, my garden grew much larger while I was unemployed. God had made an Eden for me in the midst of my desert. Though my troubles did not disappear, I knew the Lord had provided me with a small place where I could go and find "joy and gladness."

We all experience wandering in the wilderness during certain times in our lives. Other people describe these wilderness experiences as the wintertime of the soul. There are times of spiritual dryness or times when crisis hits our families like a violent winter storm. During these times, the image of God comforting all the "waste places" of his people is like a precious jewel. Isaiah 51:3 assures us of the Lord's comforting presence, which makes an Eden out of our personal desert places and transforms the winter with promises of spring.

Exercise:

Our own gardens are living reminders that God is with us, even in winter. The plants and flowers may have lost their leaves or blooms, but deep inside they are still nourished and fed until spring arrives again. Winter may make the landscape look like a "waste place," but God gives our gardens what they need to survive.

Week 44

Use the Outer Garden section to make a pencil sketch of your garden in winter. Don't worry—nobody else will see your sketch. As you draw, look for the beauty of your garden now cloaked in winter.

Reread Isaiah 51:3. Keep the sketch you made of your garden open before you. Sit quietly for fifteen minutes and reflect on the following questions and use the Inner Garden section to record your reflections.

❧ How is the Lord comforting me this winter?

❧ (If you are experiencing a wilderness time in your inner or outer life now): Is God creating an Eden for me? If so, describe this garden. If not, remember that God is with you even though it doesn't seem like it. Spend time this week asking the Lord to comfort you, to show you signs of life and promise that spring will come again. Ask God to create a garden in your desert.

Lord, as you comforted Zion, I pray you comfort me. This winter, let me find signs of your abundant life in my inner garden, strengthening me until spring. In Christ's name. Amen. ❧

Outer Garden

_____

_____

_____

_____

_____

_____

_____

_____

Inner Garden

_____

_____

_____

_____

_____

_____

_____

_____

Winter

Happy are those who . . .
delight . . . in the law of
the LORD,
and on his law they
meditate day and night.
They are like trees planted
by streams of water,
which yield their fruit in
its season,
and their leaves do not
wither.

PSALM 1:1*a*, 2–3 NRSV

I once returned from a three-day business trip to find that one of my favorite scented pelargoniums had fallen off the deck. Its pot had shattered on the asphalt below where high winds had blown it. The poor pelargonium looked dead: its roots were exposed and dry, many of its little branches had broken, most of the leaves were dead and brown. I was about to throw the plant away when instinct told me to hydrate the roots. I took it inside and placed the plant in a vase filled with water. I decided to leave it there for a few days and see whether there were any signs of life.

When I checked the plant again three days later, I saw tiny new leaf buds. So I repotted the plant and cut off all the dead branches and leaves. I was pleased to find a healthy, growing, though much smaller, pelargonium. It now flourishes on my deck once again.

Winter is a wonderful time to hydrate our spiritual roots by meditating on Scripture. Our gardens are asleep until spring. The cold and dark days often prevent us from many outdoor activities. And after all the hustle and bustle of the holidays, it's sometimes easy to feel spiritually drained and dry. The psalmist sings that the one who meditates on God's law day and night is like a tree that never knows winter, planted as it is by streams of water. When we drink from the Scripture's living stream, our souls experience new growth, and spring blooms inside us during the coldest winter.

Week 45

Exercise:

Bring a bit of spring inside during the winter. Treat yourself to fresh-cut flowers throughout the cold months. Use the Outer Garden section to list your favorite flowers, and refer to this list before going to the florist. Let the flowers remind you that the God of all living things is with you even during the coldest season.

Identify the best time to meditate on your favorite Bible verses. For example, I am a morning person, so mornings are usually best for me. You may also want to choose a time when the house is relatively quiet and find a room that provides you with some privacy. Then select two or three of your favorite Bible verses and write them down in the Inner Garden section. Meditate on these verses for thirty minutes. This is not Bible study, which primarily instructs the mind. Meditating on Scripture is focusing on just a few verses within your heart, opening up your soul to enjoy the presence of God. Have your flowers as well as your Bible with you. If possible, continue this practice throughout the winter.

Lord God, let my spiritual roots sink deep into your word. As I meditate on Scripture, refresh my spirit, renew my soul, and strengthen me for the work you are calling me to do this winter. In Jesus' name. Amen. ❧

Outer Garden

_____

_____

_____

_____

_____

_____

_____

_____

_____

_____

Inner Garden

_____

_____

_____

_____

_____

_____

_____

_____

_____

Winter

Look at the birds of the air; they neither sow nor reap nor gather into barns, and yet your heavenly Father feeds them. Are you not of more value than they?

MATTHEW 6:26 NRSV

Matthew 6:26 is perhaps my favorite verse in Scripture. In the preceding verses Jesus told us not to worry about what we shall eat or wear. He pointed to the lilies in the field and the birds of the air to show how our heavenly Father provides for us. We are valuable to God, of even more value than the birds or lilies in which our Father delights.

I find that during the winter I especially fall prey to anxiety. When the weather is bad and I can't get out and work in my garden, it's sometimes easy to slip into worrying. My favorite thing to worry over is money, regardless of how much I have in my checking account. When the days are dark and short, sometimes I forget how valuable, how precious I am to God. At the root of my anxiety over money is the sinful belief gnawing in my heart that I am worthless. Turning to this verse, I learn again that I am invaluable to God. I look out my window at the birds with a renewed perspective about God's love and providence—and I am grateful.

Exercise:

Our gardens can still be a source of wonder and pleasure even in winter. The best way to make them so is by installing a bird feeder. Winter is the time birds most need help with finding enough food to survive. Feeding and watching birds is fun, and they are a great reminder of Matthew 6:26.

Week 46

If you don't already have one, obtain a bird feeder. They come in all sizes, and with a little shopping you can certainly find one to fit your needs. I hang my bird feeder at my window so I can watch and identify the birds easily. You may want to put yours out in your winter garden, but put it somewhere within sight from inside the house. If the feeder is set at a distance, keep a pair of binoculars near the window so you can get a good look at the birds. To add to the pleasure of watching birds at your feeder, you may want to purchase a field guide to help you identify birds in your area. Keep it handy, near your binoculars.

Spend some time observing the birds that come to your feeder. Record the birds you see in the Outer Garden section.

In the Inner Garden section, list any sources of anxiety or worries you may have experienced lately. After each item on your list, write Matthew 6:26. As you watch the birds flying to and from your feeder, see them as little angels, taking your worries and cares away to God. It may help to pray the following prayer.

Heavenly Father, you have told me I am more valuable to you than the birds of the air. May each little bird fly away with one of my worries. And may I find peace in knowing that you take care of me as you take care of every bird that comes to my garden. In Jesus' name. Amen. ❧

Outer Garden

_____

_____

_____

_____

_____

_____

_____

_____

Inner Garden

_____

_____

_____

_____

_____

_____

_____

_____

Winter

May those who sow in tears reap with shouts of joy.

PSALM 126:5 NRSV

Psalm 126:5 is one of the most beautiful blessings in all of Scripture. Our pain and suffering here in this life has meaning and does not go unnoticed by God. We sow our tears like seeds in our gardens. We nurture the tears we plant in the soil of hope, shed on them the light of faith, and water them with the passing of time. Finally, our tears bring forth life, and we reap their fruit with "shouts of joy."

In suffering this winter, let us remember our gardens. Let us count our tears as seeds for sowing. Let us be faithful gardeners of our pain, knowing that summer will come to us once again and we *will* reap with shouts of joy to the Lord.

In joy this winter, let us also remember our gardens. Let us be faithful gardeners of our joy. Let us give thanks for the abundance we have reaped and raise loud shouts of joy to the Lord.

Week 47

Exercise:

If you experience any pain this week, record your suffering in the Inner Garden section. Sow your tears there. When you've finished, write Psalm 126:5 at the end. Repeat this verse to yourself every time you feel your eyes brim with tears.

If you experience joy this week, record your joy in the Outer Garden section. Especially note whether the joy you are experiencing now began during a time of sorrow. Then "reap with shouts of joy." Invite a friend or two for coffee and a time of prayer and thanksgiving.

My God, you are the Great Gardener. Take my tears and plant them in your heart until such time you deem right that I reap in joy. In Jesus' name. Amen.

Outer Garden

Inner Garden

Winter

. . . *The fruit of the*
Spirit is love, joy, peace,
patience, kindness,
generosity, faithfulness,
gentleness, and
self-control.

GALATIANS 5:22–23*a*
NRSV

Winter, when fruit and flowers are gone from our gardens, is a good time to explore our inner gardens. There we will find the Holy Spirit at work cultivating fruit in us that will never spoil. Now is the time to walk with the Spirit in our inner gardens to see what is growing there.

Galatians 5:22 has always been one of my favorite verses because the fruit of the Spirit is so *beautiful*. When I meet another Christian whose inner garden is clearly filled with the fruit of kindness, I see a beautiful person regardless of her outward appearance. The kindness she shows to the world is really the Holy Spirit at work making the world a more beautiful place, showing forth the presence of God. Even the spiritual fruit of self-control adds beauty to our world because in self-control God makes his presence known.

Exercise:

Our gardens may be asleep, but winter still shows the beauty of God's creation. Take a walk in winter. If you can, walk for an hour through your neighborhood or in a park. Choose a day that is not so inclement as to make taking a walk uncomfortable. On your walk, look for anything that shows the beauty of God's creation. It may be the cold, crisp air, fresh snow, bare branches against a brilliant winter sky, or the way ice forms on windows. Take this book with you and jot down what you see in the Outer Garden section.

Week 48

When you come home, settle down with a nice hot cup of tea or cocoa. As you sip your hot drink, reflect on the kind of fruit the Holy Spirit is producing in your life—it is a sign of the beauty of God's creation and presence in you. Ask yourself:

ꝏ Which fruit in Galatians 5:22-23 do I see in my life?

ꝏ How has this fruit enriched my experience of the Holy Spirit?

ꝏ How has the fruit of the Spirit in my life touched the lives of others? (Be as concrete as possible.)

ꝏ What fruit shall I ask the Spirit in prayer to produce in me?

Record your thoughts in the Inner Garden section.

Holy Spirit, I thank you for the fruit you are producing in my life. May I always show forth your presence in the world, touching other lives with your beauty and light. Help me to continually rejoice in you, enjoying your presence within me and in the lives of others. In Jesus' name. Amen. ꝏ

Outer Garden

_____
_____
_____
_____
_____
_____
_____
_____

Inner Garden

_____
_____
_____
_____
_____
_____
_____
_____

Winter

*Though the fig tree does
not blossom,
and no fruit is on the
vines;
though the produce of the
olive fails
and the fields yield no
food;
though the flock is cut off
from the fold
and there is no herd in the
stalls,
yet I will rejoice in the
LORD;
I will exult in the God of
my salvation.*

HABAKKUK 3:17–18
NRSV

During the depth of winter, we may feel cut off from many sources of emotional and spiritual nourishment. Work in our gardens is limited or impossible. We may struggle with occasional bouts of "cabin fever." The days are short: dawn is long in coming and night falls quickly. So light seems rare. Around the middle of February, many of us and our loved ones may experience mid-winter blues.

Sometimes this wintry lack of emotional nourishment has an impact on our spiritual lives. The cold darkness of winter seems to dim the light of God. Habakkuk wrote about a very real lack of spiritual nourishment using an image of great physical deprivation—Israel cut off from God, awaiting an attack by their enemies. Mid-winter may also make us feel as though the nourishing warmth of God is far away, and we are left alone to battle depression.

While Habakkuk wrote realistically about the lack of spiritual nourishment, he also wrote about how to find God again, "Yet I will rejoice in the Lord; I will exult in the God of my salvation." We can lighten the long, dark months of winter by rejoicing with and celebrating the God of our salvation. Joyful celebration in God our Savior nourishes us emotionally and spiritually and makes spring bloom in the middle of winter.

Week 49

Exercise:

To fight the mid-winter blues and spiritual doldrums, give an old-fashioned hymn-sing. Invite friends to a potluck, and tell everyone that after dinner you will sing hymns together. Borrow several hymnals from your church. Let your guests call out their favorite hymns and spend an hour or so rejoicing together in the Lord. Record the evening's experience in your Outer Garden section.

To continue the battle against the winter darkness, include in your daily schedule a time to read aloud from Psalms. Look through Psalms and choose verses of praise, such as Psalms 1, 133–136, 144–150. Each day read one aloud, then choose a verse, memorize it, and carry it in your heart all day. Repeat the verse to yourself throughout the day, especially when you feel the mid-winter blues setting in. Record the verses you memorize in the Inner Garden section.

Lord, though the winter days may be dark, though you may seem far away sometimes, yet I will praise you. May your Holy Spirit cause me to rejoice in you. Help me to reach out and join with other Christians to celebrate your abiding presence. In Jesus' name. Amen.

Outer Garden

_____
_____
_____
_____
_____
_____
_____

Inner Garden

_____
_____
_____
_____
_____
_____
_____

Winter

For there is hope for a
*   tree,*
if it is cut down, that it
*   will sprout again,*
and that its shoots will
*   not cease.*
Though its root grows old
*   in the earth,*
and its stump dies in the
*   ground,*
yet at the scent of water it
*   will bud*
and put forth branches
*   like a young plant.*
    JOB 14:7–9 NRSV

Many gardeners have had the experience of cutting down an unwanted or diseased tree. Once the tree is cut down there is the problem of the stump; trees don't die easily. My landlord once cut down a tree that was growing too close to my cottage. The tree also blocked out so much sunlight that little could grow in his garden. He did not dig up the stump (a huge project!) but left it in the ground. Each spring it sends out new branches with tiny, tender leaves.

Many of us have experienced significant loss in our lives—the death of a family member; the break-up of a marriage; an abrupt end to a career; a long, dear friendship ending bitterly. Some of us may even have experienced the loss of a home through natural disaster. We are left feeling like a big piece of us has been cut off, the pain is so great. But though the pain is very great, God's people are not easy to kill. We are like the tree that has been cut down, whose roots continue to grow old in the earth. When, in time, we begin to accept the loss we have suffered, we begin to live again. A kind of resurrection takes place, and, like the old, battered stump, we begin to come to life again.

Week 50

Exercise:

Weather permitting, take a walk through your neighborhood or local park. Look for the stump of a tree. You may need only to go into your backyard. In wintertime, there are probably no signs of life. In the Outer Garden section describe the stump you found and where it's located. Sketch the stump and its immediate surroundings. Return to the stump periodically throughout the coming year—are there any signs of life developing?

If you've experienced a loss in your life recently, describe it briefly in the Inner Garden section. Are you able to identify any signs of healing? If so, describe that healing. If you aren't experiencing healing just now, that's all right. Write a prayer asking for healing, for a sign that the God of all life will renew your life once again.

Lord Jesus, you are the Great Healer. I run to you for help. Thank you for your healing presence in the past. I ask, O Lord, that you be with me now, that I may always know your healing touch so my life and strength will be renewed. In your name. Amen.

Outer Garden

_____
_____
_____
_____
_____
_____
_____
_____

Inner Garden

_____
_____
_____
_____
_____
_____
_____
_____

Winter

As long as the earth
endures,
seedtime and harvest,
cold and heat,
summer and winter, day
and night,
shall not cease.

GENESIS 8:22 NRSV

Gardeners work according to the seasons. We carefully listen to weather reports and watch the skies and the thermometer to know when to sow, when to reap, and when to simply sit and enjoy this beautiful part of God's creation.

The change of seasons is evidence of God's love for us. Out of God's goodness, life on earth will continue. Winter is also a sign of God's love. Depending on where we live, winter may limit what we can do in our gardens. And that is a blessing. For winter is a time of quietness and reflection, a time of "nesting" while much of the earth sleeps and waits for spring. Winter is the contemplative season. It invites us to sit by the hearth and dream about God, to shift our focus from creation to the Creator.

Week 51

Exercise:

During the winter months, block out time on your calendar to sit by the fire and simply enjoy the presence of God's company. These should be special times in addition to whatever quiet time or Bible study you may already be doing. Use your Bible, a hymnal, or your journal to help you focus on the love of the Creator. Pray, sing, or quietly review your life under the eye of God. Whatever you choose to do, even if you choose to leave your burdens with the Lord, enjoy the God who created you. Record your experience in the Inner Garden section.

Creator God, I give you thanks for winter, a sign that the earth will continue. May your Holy Spirit create in me a clean heart, filled with wonder at your abiding love. In Jesus' name. Amen.

Outer Garden

_____

_____

_____

_____

_____

_____

_____

_____

Inner Garden

_____

_____

_____

_____

_____

_____

_____

Winter

Sow for yourselves
  righteousness;
reap steadfast love;
break up your fallow
  ground;
for it is time to seek the
  LORD,
that he may come and
  rain righteousness upon
  you.

HOSEA 10:12 NRSV

Hosea used this agricultural image to call God's people to repentance and salvation. I've always thought this a good verse to remember during Lent. The Lenten season is a time of seeking the Lord by repenting of our sins and eagerly anticipating the events of Holy Week and Easter.

Of course, Lent occurs in the middle of winter. As our gardens quietly sleep, Lent is an excellent time to embark on a journey in search of God. And so we leave our gardens for a little while to take this forty-day Lenten journey. It is a journey that sows righteousness, reaps steadfast love, and breaks up the fallow ground of our hearts so that we may experience the Lord's righteousness, which comes upon us like a fresh, spring rain.

Exercise:

You may work on this exercise this week or extend it through the forty days of Lent. Our Lenten journey is a journey outward and a journey inward.

Begin by praying for God to lead you to do a special work of love. It may be volunteering in a soup kitchen; getting involved in your church in a special way; visiting the sick, elderly, or imprisoned; working at your local animal shelter; or volunteering an hour or more a week anywhere you believe God calls you to show forth his love.

Week 52

You may already be involved as a volunteer or minister in some capacity. If so, ask God to sanctify your ministry as an important part of your Lenten journey.

Once you've selected a place, negotiate to work there as your time and schedule permits. Record where you are working in the Outer Garden section. Return to this section to record your experiences there.

As you continue in your special work of love, answer the following questions in the Inner Garden section:

❧ How is this experience changing me?

❧ How is this experience showing me where I need to repent?

❧ How am I learning/experiencing God's righteousness?

❧ Where do I see God's steadfast love?

Almighty God, break up the fallow ground of my heart this Lent. Sow there the seeds of righteousness and let grow a love for you so deep and profound that all who see it may enjoy your work through me. In Jesus' name. Amen. ❧

Outer Garden

_____
_____
_____
_____
_____
_____
_____
_____
_____

Inner Garden

_____
_____
_____
_____
_____
_____
_____
_____

About the Author

Harriet Crosby is a freelance writer living in the hills of Oakland, California.